The
Extroverted
Writer

An Author's Guide to Marketing and Building a Platform

AMANDA LUEDEKE

CONTENTS

INTRODUCTION

Go ahead, say it—say the one word that publishers and agents hide behind. The word that *will* delay your writing career. The word that will be your nemesis from this day forward. Say it. I dare you.

Platform.

You're not alone in your hatred of this vague and overused moniker. When I first came on the publishing scene, I was astounded at how often this term was thrown around. You see, I came from a marketing background. For three years I had worked for major national clients, helping them launch YouTube channels and Facebook groups, blogs, websites, and apps. So, this term (the author's arch rival) meant nothing to me. In my world of social media, platform could be easily achieved. Platform was possible.

But not in publishing. Nope. In publishing, platform is mysterious and unchained. It has no simple definition, no solid qualities. Ask an agent or editor or publicist what constitutes an impressive platform, and they'll balk right in front of you. It's as though He-Who-Must-Not-Be-Named is in fact *platform* and not Lord Voldemort from the Harry Potter series.

Even worse was when the problem was compounded by a common ailment I like to call *excuses of the introverted*. Writers are artists. We're quirky, awkward, and maybe a little gun shy. We're introverts, the lot of us. And we hide behind this excuse, claiming that our introversion prevents us from reaching out, from peddling our goods, from gaining platform.

My friends, the Internet eliminated the Introvert's last excuse. The Internet is your best friend. Gone are the days of on-the-spot conversing. Banished are the times when you actually needed to be good at public speaking to get anyone to listen to you, and vanished are door-to-door sales techniques. In their place now sits a monitor and a bit of Wi-Fi, and the world is your oyster, whether you change out of those pajamas in the morning or not.

What Is Platform Anyway?

Let me break it down for you plain and simple: platform is a number. If you add together all of your Facebook fans, all of your Twitter followers, all of the people who attend your speaking engagements, and so on, you get your immediate platform.

Now, your next question (because mind reading is my part-time job) has to do with how big that number needs to be in order to attract attention.

Though this changes, and there's not a one-size-fits-all approach, publishers of nonfiction projects typically want an author to have a following (or a potential following) in the hundreds of thousands, while publishers of fiction don't need debut authors to have platforms. Of course, it goes without saying that a debut novelist *with* a solid platform will be chosen over a debut author *without* one. When this happens (and it *does* happen!), what does the platform look like? We typically view a debut author with a platform in the tens of thousands to be super solid.

Now I know what you're doing. You're panicking. You may even be crying and tearing your clothes or pajamas in frustration. STOP IT. Remember when I said I worked in marketing before publishing? Remember how platform doesn't scare me? It's because I know something that others don't.

I know how to grow a platform.

And I'm going to tell you what I know.

If you ask an editor, a publisher, a publicist, or an agent what constitutes a solid platform, they'll usually dodge the question. They'll offer vague terms while pointing out an author who has a book deal and a well-read blog. You then ask them how to *grow* a platform, and they very well might act like they didn't hear you. Why? Because they don't know. They weren't marketers. They've probably never even seen the back end of a website, let alone published a blog post. And yet the one thing they do know is that the only way to get a book deal is to magically grow this thing called platform—like it's some sort of "Jack and the Beanstalk" deal.

I realize this sounds cocky of me, as though I laugh in the face of the universe's problems, but that's not my intention. I'm simply trying to communicate that *I get it*. I know building a platform seems impossible, and oftentimes we publishing professionals, who are supposed to offer advice and guidance and direction, leave you more confused than ever when we fail to answer your questions with coherent, actionable answers.

I know this because this was how I first saw the publishing scene with my fresh, unjaded eyes. And I knew something needed to be done. For a year, I wrote about growing a platform on our company blog, but that wasn't enough. My posts were too difficult to search and reference, and I was limited by reasonable word count and readability.

So, this book was born.

More than anything, this book is a bunch of ideas and rules, all categorized and labeled (hopefully quite well) in a shiny package. If I could encourage you to do anything while reading this book, it would be to jot down ten things that are doable for you. That's it! You may feel like information is coming at you rapidly, and some parts of it you're going to brush off while scratching your head in confusion at others. But there will be parts of it that make complete sense whether you're a social media newbie or long-time pro, publishing veteran or new writer. Those are the parts for YOU, my friend. Those are the parts you need to focus on. This is your tool guide to growing your platform.

I bring you this little book in hopes to break the spell, provide answers to questions, and make platform more of a worthy foe than an insurmountable obstacle.

And by the end of it, you might even be saying its name aloud.

1
KNOW YOUR AUDIENCE

There's a common saying that marketing is nothing more than finding your audience and standing in front of it. Sounds simple enough, but what is simple can quickly become complex. For example, let's say you're an expert toymaker. What audience or market loves toys? Why children, of course. That seems to be a no-brainer, but there's a catch. If you were standing in front of a first grade classroom with your epic set of robot action figures and dolls, how many of those children would be able to pay you right then and there? How many carry around wads of cash or credit cards? And how many of their parents are going to hunt you down to make the transaction after the children have gone home and raved and whined about your toys?

This is why the idea of standing in front of your audience doesn't always work as well as we'd like. In this instance, the children who really loved the toys are going to go home and ask for them. Eventually, the parents may follow through on those requests, but it gets even more interesting. In this day and age, where do parents shop?

Chances are they'll go online. They'll research the product

until they know whether the purchase is worthwhile, and only then will they buy.

This is why online marketing is so effective. Only online are you able to be in multiple places at once, targeting both children *and* their parents with a strategy that leads them directly to a purchase page within seconds. Children are no longer waiting for a toy commercial to come on the TV in order to show Mom or Dad. They are no longer looking forward to the weekend when they might go to the mall and their parents might remember to pick up your product. You cut through all of these potential roadblocks by going online and knowing how to tailor your message to your audience.

If I were to give a list of rules for marketing and promotion, I'd maintain the old marketing adage and agree that the first step should be to find your audience. And while that's clearly the tip of the iceberg, it's a worthwhile start.

Your Audience

If I were to ask you who the audience is for your book, there's a very good chance that you'll answer with something ridiculous like, "Men, women, children...really anyone looking for a great story!" You may even take it a step further and realize that such a statement is a bit wild and would be much more acceptable if you provided proof. So, you may say something like, "Well, my eighty-year-old mother read it and loved it, and so did my teenage grandchildren! It's really a timeless story."

And here's where I level with you. I deal with this kind of stuff all the time. Just because your mom said that you're the best singer in the world doesn't mean you should forgo college and try out for *American Idol.* And the same goes for writing books. It's these types of people who struggle the most with marketing their books, because they aren't able to look at them objectively. They aren't able to recognize that while their families may love them and want to be supportive, a story about a "fifty-year-old woman who rediscovers life" is not going to be on a teen's must-read list.

The Theater Test

My parents really wanted to see the movie *The Iron Lady*, a biopic about Margaret Thatcher. So, the three of us went to the theater and took our seats. I really enjoyed the movie and found it quite moving, so much so that I would probably recommend it to my friends if the subject came up.

Right after the movie ended and the lights came back on, I remember standing up and realizing that I was younger than everyone else in the room by at least twenty years (I was twenty-eight at the time). Not only that, but I realized that almost everyone there was with his or her spouse. And they were all white people, probably conservatives (they had that look about them), and they seemed to fall in the middle or upper middle class.

Okay, so basically, they were all clones of my parents.

If *The Iron Lady* were a book, many new authors would want to say that it appeals to young and old, conservatives and moderates alike. They would back up their claim and say, "See! There is a twenty-eight-year-old libertarian among the viewers!"

I would have skewed their data wildly, and they would have loved it. But I was not the target audience for that movie. Yes, I enjoyed it, and yes, I would speak highly of it. But those who were most willing to purchase tickets fell into a very distinct category, and the moviemakers would have been silly to think otherwise.

This is what I mean when I say *know your audience*. Have the ability to filter out those that skew your numbers and focus on what is blatantly in front of you.

Why do this? Because knowing your audience makes it so much easier to market your book.

The previews that aired before *The Iron Lady* were all targeted at that specific audience. They were all either feel-good stories (Nicholas Sparks-type movies) or patriotic flicks.

Moviemakers of those movies knew their target audience. They knew they'd be attending *The Iron Lady*, so that's where they put their marketing dollars and efforts. And it worked. (My parents oohed and aahed at each preview.)

Your first task before you do anything else is to find your audience.

Breaking the Rules

Some books take off. Some books cross audiences and truly become cultural favorites that are loved by young and old, rich and poor, and individuals of all races and nationalities alike.

But every book starts in a single genre and with a single audience. *Every* book.

This is why publishing houses have multiple imprints. Let's take HarperCollins, for example. Voyager is its speculative fiction line, HarperTeen is one of its YA lines, Avon is its romance line, Zondervan and Thomas Nelson are its inspirational lines, and so on. When agents sell books, we target the right imprint for it. When Joanna Stampfel-Volpe sold Veronica Roth's debut novel *Divergent,* she sold it to Katherine Tegan Books, one of HarperCollins' YA imprints. *Divergent* has been enjoyed by teens and adults of both genders. But it had to start somewhere, and at its core, it's a YA novel.

The same goes for my author Jill Williamson. She writes inspirational teen fiction that is enjoyed by readers of all ages and religious backgrounds. But I would never approach Katherine Tegan Books with Jill's novels. Instead, the deals I've done for her have been with Zondervan. It's still under the HarperCollins umbrella, but it's a better match for the core of Jill's readership.

How to Find Your Audience

All right, enough theory. Let's get practical. How do you take a book that is loved by everyone and your mother and find its basic readership—those who are most inclined to shell out fifteen dollars to buy it (or those who are most inclined to get their parents to shell out fifteen dollars)?

First, you must identify other movies or books or plays that are similar to your work. So, go to the bookstore or get online and put on your researcher jeans.

The first similarity should be genre. Match mysteries with mysteries, cozy mysteries with cozy mysteries, police procedurals with police procedurals, and so on. **Pay specific attention to where these books are shelved.** For example, Nancy Drew is a mystery series, but it's shelved over in the children's section, making it a juvenile mystery fiction series. You wouldn't compare readers of Nancy Drew with readers of Agatha Christie (even though Agatha Christie readers most likely read Nancy Drew in their youth).

The second similarity should have to do with main characters. Match female, upper teen leads with other female, upper teen leads. Match male, mid-fifties leads with other male, mid-fifties leads. This will help you narrow your comparison search. Like the Nancy Drew series, the Hardy Boys is a similar mystery series for children, but it has male protagonists. Therefore, if your children's mystery had a female lead, you could exclude the Hardy Boys from your list of *similar titles*. The two series are near identical in many ways, but their audiences are different. You need to only concern yourself with finding the best possible matches you can.

Once you've come up with a list of projects that are similar to your own, **try out one of these methods to identify and profile your readership**. (Yes, we're getting uber technical at this point.)

1. Stalk people in bookstores. Believe it or not, this is a real marketing research tactic, though in the real world it has a much more hi-tech term. But let's just call it what it is. This tactic, should you choose to accept it, involves going to a bookstore and watching the shopping habits of readers. You can either keep an eye on an entire genre section to see which books various types of people tend to pick up, or you can watch specific titles. Pay attention to age, race, socio-economic status, and any hobbies that may be clearly visible. This method may take a long time, because you need a large sampling before you can begin to pull trends.

2. Stalk moviegoers. This tactic, should you choose to accept it, involves doing exactly what I did at *The Iron Lady* (see above). Find a movie that is similar to your book and pay attention to the types of people in the seats. *This method works only for fiction.*

3. Stalk people online. Most authors and/or books have people online talking about them—from Goodreads to Yahoo! Groups, to old school message boards and forums. If you're good with Google, you can very easily tap into these groups and create simple reader profiles. This is a great method for fiction and nonfiction authors alike.

Target reader profiles typically end up looking something like these (each represents an entirely different reader group):

- Women, ages 30–55. Most likely SAHMs (stay-at-home moms) or WAHMs (work-at-home moms). Hobbies include baking, crafting, scrapbooking.

- Men, ages 35–60. The "business traveler." Corporate workers, who appreciate a high-action thriller (military or otherwise) to take their minds off their responsibilities.

- Teen girls, ages 16–18. More artistic than athletic. Hobbies include dating and relationships.

Take the time to research your target readership/market and craft a simple profile similar to the ones above. Feel free to be as detailed as you want, even going so far as to create a private pinboard on Pinterest for you to keep images of who your reader is and what his or her life constitutes.

Do this, and only then will you be ready to grow your platform.

2
KNOW YOUR GOALS

You've heard it before that if you really want to impress an agent, make sure you have three things: a great idea, great writing, and a great platform.

But let's be honest, either you're born with a knack for words or you're not.

Either a great idea drops into your head one day, or it doesn't.

But platform doesn't happen by chance. Platform is all about hard work.

It's funny that we dedicate entire conferences, workshops, and critique groups to the very components that we have the least control over, but the third component—the one that really *can* be taught into existence—gets constantly ignored. You can't make great writers out of bad writers, and not a single classic American novel was written by following a novel-writing template.

This really bugs me, because we've turned platform into this mysterious entity that's somehow more difficult to achieve than writing a best seller. Somewhere along the line we've decided using social media is more nebulous than developing a plot destined for the silver screen and that growing a readership as an unpublished author is more far-fetched than an agent offering on-the-spot representation.

In my never-ending quest to pull platform out of the doghouse, I'm going to spill the goods and answer the question that every author asks: What do impressive social media stats look like?

Hold on, it's going to be a bumpy ride.

The Numbers

Solid author platforms come in the **tens or hundreds of thousands**.

Let's get more specific.

If you have a **website or blog**, your **monthly unique visitor count should be at least 30,000**.

If you have a **Twitter** account, your followers should be at least **5,000**.

If you have a **Facebook** group, your following should be pushing **5,000**.

If you're a **public speaker**, you should **speak at least 30 times a year**, and you should shoot for a **total audience number of at least 10,000**.

If you write for **e-zines and e-publications** on a regular basis, you should have your words in front of at least **100,000 readers per month**.

If you write for **print publications** on a regular basis, you should have your words in front of at least **100,000 readers per quarter**.

If you've **e-published**, your sales in the first year should be in the **hundreds of thousands for a $0.99 e-book** and in the **tens or hundreds of thousands for a $2.99 e-book**.

If you've **POD (print on demand) published**, your sales within the first year should be at least **5,000 copies**.

Intimidated yet? I know I am. These numbers aren't easy to achieve.

The time and effort required to grow such a following

might have you envisioning yourself with an impressive platform sometime in the year 2030. You may even be thinking about how you don't have a single sales bone in your body. You're an artist, after all, and an *introverted* artist at that. Those qualities don't always make for the most sociable, friendly, outgoing, spin-doctoring bunch.

So, what's the secret? How can these numbers be achieved?

Before you delete all the Word documents containing your manuscripts and then jump off a cliff, **there are a few things to keep in mind**:

1. Platform is a grand total. Add up all of your numbers in each of the listed categories and see what you have. If you're nearing the tens of thousands, you're off to a great start, even if your Twitter numbers are pathetic and you haven't attempted half of the things on the list. The idea isn't that you have to do all of these things extremely well. You don't even have to do *all* of these things. You can achieve success by doing a few of them *really* well or all of them *somewhat* well. The choice is yours, but I'd personally opt for the more focused approach. I am, after all, only one person, and my time is limited and precious.

2. Fiction authors could cut these numbers in half. Fiction is a different ball game. An impressive debut novelist can have a Twitter following of 2,500 and a blog readership of 10,000 unique visitors per month and still look impressive to the right editor.

3. It's a process. No one, not even Justin Bieber, achieved success without actually doing anything. It takes time to build relationships and garner a following. You're not doing yourself any favors by getting down on yourself for having only 100 blog readers after blogging religiously for only three months. You need to allow yourself time. And by that, I mean years. I've been an agent since 2010, and I'm still working at getting my name out there. Success doesn't happen overnight. If you feel like that doesn't apply to you or you wonder if it's all worth it, then you're probably in the wrong business.

4. There are always exceptions to the rule. *BUT, AMANDA!!! I know someone who knows someone who just got a book deal, and they don't even know what Twitter is!* Yes, this happens. And sure, there's a chance it could happen to you. In fact, I hope it does! But like I said before, having the right story written at the right time and pitched to the right editor or agent involves a lot of luck. Platform is about hard work and creating something that simply cannot be ignored. It really is the one thing that you can control.

When your book sells really well because of the platform you built, and your publisher wants to do even more books with you, all of this will be worth it. Trust me.

3
KNOW HOW TO USE THIS BOOK

Now that you know what to shoot for in terms of numbers, you may have dusted off your blog and your Facebook group and opened an old manuscript that you're thinking of e-publishing.

Before you go further, I implore you to SLOW THE HECK DOWN.

Most authors, when embarking on a quest to tackle the Platform Monster, treat it like spaghetti. They throw everything at the wall to see what sticks. They start a Facebook group, a Twitter account, a blog, a website, a Goodreads account, a newsletter, and on and on and on until they feel they have all of the possible platform-building areas covered.

And then they're surprised when nothing happens, when their Facebook group hovers around 50 "Likes" (most of which are family or friends), when their Twitter account has more spam followers than real followers, and when their website stats don't climb above 30 visits a day. They're surprised by this, because they're doing everything they're supposed to do and nothing is working. And more than anything, they're exhausted. They've spread themselves so thin they can barely keep track of what was said where. At this point, most give up. They tried their best, and it didn't work.

But platform is nothing like spaghetti. It's more like placing dominoes in a row. Select one social media channel out of the dozens available. Pour all you have into that one outlet—your time, your creativity, your resources (and yes, sometimes your money). Stick with it, and when it starts to grow, add something else.

You'll realize that this new outlet is much easier to grow because you have your foundation. Keep slowly building your online presence until you're comfortable, NOT until you're overworked and exhausted. Then, when it takes off, it will ALL take off. It's just like how hitting one domino amidst a bunch of perfectly placed dominoes sets off a chain reaction.

This book is categorized by social media channels. There's a section on websites, one on blogs, one on Facebook, and a section on Twitter. These are the most-used outlets. Then there's a section on miscellaneous outlets, such as Pinterest and Goodreads.

For newbies, instead of treating the book like a checklist, I encourage you to read through it, and then let it sit. Maybe open a Facebook or Twitter account if you haven't already and poke around. Take time to figure out what you're comfortable with, and then choose one thing out of them all that you will focus on.

For more experienced social media users, I stand behind my advice in the Introduction to come away with ten things that are do-able for you and your current online presence.

In other words, it doesn't matter how experienced or inexperienced you are.

You may be starting from scratch.

You may have a number of abandoned social media efforts.

Or you may be a social media guru in need of a bit of direction or a few fresh ideas

Regardless, this book is for you. And taking it one step at a time will ensure success.

4
WEBSITES

We're going to start with websites because **this is the one thing that every author or aspiring author should have**.

Why Published Authors Need Websites

The website is the most crucial component because it brings everything together.

Let's say you're most comfortable using Facebook. Therefore, you develop your Facebook page and start getting "Likes." You utilize its Photos and Notes features and are consistent about posting to it. Eventually, you realize you can handle more. So, you venture into Twitter. After that, you launch a YouTube channel and then a blog. Soon you have many different social media channels going at once, and when people ask where to find you online, you rattle off your Facebook URL, your Twitter handle, your Tumblr URL, and your YouTube channel name. Not the most effective, is it? You need a central hub where they all link together.

Enter the website.

A great website will give fans a one-stop place where *they* can decide how they want to follow you. Do they want to subscribe to your blog? Follow you on Twitter? Be notified through e-mail?

A great website will have all of the author's social media sites easily accessible from the home page. We're talking his or her blog, Facebook, Twitter, and so on. This increases the likelihood that a user who happens to be dropping by for a quick check-in will be encouraged to interact with you in a medium with which they're most comfortable.

A great website will become your go-to reference when people (including industry professionals) ask where they can find you online, not to mention it screams of professionalism. And when was that ever a bad thing?

Why Unpublished Authors Need Websites

It's pretty obvious why *published* authors need websites. In an age when celebrities are more accessible than ever through Twitter, Facebook, and YouTube, authors need to follow suit. If I can Tweet my favorite actor or band and get a response, I should be able to interact with my favorite mid-list author.

Random note: I've found the typical response to this argument is that celebrities can pay workers to be active on Twitter and Facebook on their behalf. Sure, sometimes that's the case, but how is that a good excuse for an author to not have an online presence? Celebrities can also afford dieticians and chefs, but that doesn't mean us regular folk, who can't afford those things, don't have to eat well.

As an additional answer to this misled logic, I guarantee that when workers are hired to handle a celebrity's social media it's because that celebrity is either simply too busy (e.g., the President of the United States) or too unfamiliar with how to navigate the Internet. Younger celebrities view Twitter and Facebook to be as much a part of life as we do, and it doesn't take much effort to snap a photo and upload it to Twitter (ask Miley Cyrus, Zach Braff, or Ashton Kutcher) or write a blog post to your fans (ask George R. R. Martin).

But what about the *unpublished* author? What value does having a website provide if it can't showcase a published work?

Let's look at the business- and platform-related effects of having a website:

1. **A website tells potential agents and editors you're serious about your career.** Believe it or not, some authors aren't looking to make a career out of writing. Sure, they may be very serious about getting the *one* book they've written published, but after that, they're done. They don't have any more stories in them, or they aren't committed to the long term. Having a website tells industry professionals that you're in this for the long haul, and you're willing to invest some money to make it happen.

2. **A website tells potential agents and editors that you aren't afraid of using the web to promote yourself.** Most authors don't know how to navigate social media. Having a website dispels those fears for agents and editors when considering your project. Even though most authors have someone else build or maintain their sites, it still tells us that you're willing to find help in order to develop an online presence.

3. **A website gives potential agents/editors an avenue through which they can learn more about who you are.** Query letters can be a bit impersonal, but a website with a full About the Author section, blog, photos, etc., gives agents like me an opportunity to do some snooping without committing to the relationship. In this business, we work with people we like, and if your website is able to give us warm, fuzzy feelings about you as a person, you're more likely to make it through the "creep check." I've had editors contact me after a conference, wondering about so-and-so unpublished author. They met the author at the conference, got a good impression, and then found themselves snooping around the author's website. They then contact me to see if I'm either working with the unpublished author or am aware of them. Pretty cool, right?

How to Get Started

If you're looking to build the website yourself (whether because of cost issues or creative control), there are a number of options—sometimes *too* many options—so I figured I'd break it down for you:

BEGINNERS (those who have zero web-building experience) should consider utilizing services such as Intuit.com or 1and1.com. These websites exist to help people and small businesses build and maintain websites. They have lots of templates that you can choose from, so there's no need to worry about design, and building them is generally as easy as dropping in your content and dragging things around the interface. They typically offer domain services so that you can purchase your domain directly from them as opposed to going through a third party. (Your domain is whatever you choose for your web address. For MacGregor Literary, our website's address is MacGregorLiterary.com. We purchased this domain when we set up our website.)

Another perk is that these service sites typically have very helpful and accessible customer service teams. Should you ever get in a bind, you'll have someone to contact who is familiar with the product.

INTERMEDIATE users (those who've dabbled in blogging and either know a bit of HTML or are at least familiar with how it works) should consider building their own sites through WordPress or another similar blogging platform that is user-friendly. The web is full of pre-made templates/themes that you can purchase from online providers. Just make sure that the theme you purchase is:

1. Compatible with your interface (e.g., WordPress templates should only be used on a WordPress site)

2. Offers what you need it to offer (If you have big dreams for an image scroller or videos on your home page, make sure that your template of choice has these capabilities.)

A great WordPress theme site is ElegantThemes.com, but you can find many more by Googling the name of your platform and then "themes."

EXPERT users (those who know HTML, CSS, etc.) probably don't need much help from me in this department, so I won't say much other than YOU ROCK.

Remember, you will have to pay for a domain name and for server usage at the very least. If you're just getting started, this will probably cost you about $100 per year. The website-building sites I mentioned, such as Intuit, will have a monthly fee associated with them, but they will most likely absorb the domain and server usage costs. This is why I recommend building a site through WordPress and other similar platforms if you can, because they're really a one-stop shop. You can get everything you need through them, including great customization, and it's usually much less expensive than going through a provider or specialist.

Getting Fancy

If you're really serious about putting your best foot forward and coming off as professional as possible (highly recommended!), you should plan to hire out a bit of design work. Designers will cost you anywhere from $200–$20,000, depending on what you want to have done and how experienced they are. Designers who are also web builders will cost even more, as they're able to implement their designs.

Personally, unless you're a bestselling author, I don't see the need to shell out more than $1,000 on your site. Spending $500 would be ideal. So, if $100 goes to the basic start-up costs (domain, server, etc.), then set aside $300 or so and find a designer who is either fresh out of college or recommended by the head of the graphic design department at your local university. Hire the student to create a masthead (the banner thingy at the top of the website) and possibly a logo (if that fits what you're going for). You will need to provide them with specs (or maybe you can luck out and find a designer who is willing to go into your website and figure out what is needed), but they'll be able to provide you with a professional-looking design that will make your entire site look and feel unique. This is totally worth it.

Some things to keep in mind when hiring a designer:

- Ask to see previous work. You want to make sure his or her design style appeals to you.

- Ask to speak with past clients. You want to get a feel for how easy he or she is to work with and how quickly or slowly he or she can produce.

- Be sure to have a contract drawn up. You don't want to go into this on a handshake. You want something you can use for accountability.

- They may ask for some money up front. This is fine, but don't give more than half. I'd say 25% is a good deposit.

- Follow through on your end of the deal. If the designer did the work, then you have to pay him or her, regardless of whether you LIKE the work. Remember, it's your job to communicate what you're looking for. Be sure to provide examples of websites that you love and be as clear about direction as you can, while still trusting his or her designer expertise.

- Listen to your designer. Clients have a tendency to think they know best. They seem to think that anyone can design and they could easily whip up a great masthead themselves if they had the right software. But remember that your designer has been trained, and he or she knows the rules of design that may not make sense to you. Trust is key.

For a good laugh, check out ClientsFromHell.net. And whatever you do, don't end up as a story on that blog!

Content Is King – Unpublished Authors
What is there to say when you don't have a book, signings to advertise, releases to blog about, or characters that readers

love? Most unpublished authors who are determined to launch a site end up staring at empty text boxes, wondering what the heck to say. What do people want to know about when you're a no-name, aspiring author?

Fear not! I have solutions!

When building a website as an unpublished author, your goal should be to **provide editors, agents, and the publishing world with a better picture of who you are and what you're about**. Keep this in mind as you create and tweak your content. But, more specifically, you'll need:

1. An awesome masthead. The masthead, or banner, is the chunk of pretty design that sits at the top of most websites. If you note Susan Sleeman's masthead, found at susansleeman.com, she not only has her author name front and center, but she has a tagline and really awesome buttons that link to her social media. It pulls people in. This is the type of masthead you want!

2. A great author picture. Believe it or not, but most authors are afraid to put their photos online. And it always boils down to one of two reasons: they either feel uncomfortable with the way they look or they believe it's self-serving to promote themselves instead of their work. This is where I do a MAJOR eye roll. How can a publisher trust you to promote your book with in-store appearances, Skype interviews, blog hops, and other such devices if you're too shy and introverted to post something as harmless as a photo?

3. An informative About page. No, we don't want your life story, but five or so paragraphs of your journey as a writer, parent, physical therapist, and whatever else life has thrown at you is very valuable. But before you write, be sure to shed any journalistic qualities you may have picked up in college or the workplace. Yes, the About section is a pure regurgitation of information, but you want it to be fun and lively. And you want it to reflect your writer's voice. If you're a fan of *The Pioneer Woman* (Google it if you're into fun, homey blogs!), take a look at the About page for inspiration. It's one of the best

I've ever seen.

If you're a nonfiction author, this is also the place where you prove why you're qualified to write about your topic. Work experience, education, published essays or articles—these things should be highlighted in some way that piques interest and positions you as an expert in your field.

4. A Contact page. Time to drop your online privacy inhibitions! A Contact page just isn't complete without contact information. Your e-mail address is a must.

Now, if you're a nonfiction writer, then you really need to beef up this page. Include your postal address and even a phone number for people to book speaking events. You want it to be as easy for people to contact you as possible.

5. A blog. Okay, so you have the crucial information covered, but where do you get to show your skills? Linking your blog to your website (or even having it *live* on your site) is a great way to allow industry professionals the chance to scope out your writing talent. If you do this, your blog needs to be updated on a regular basis, it needs to hit your target readership, and it needs to be well written. For tips on blogging, jump ahead to the blogging chapter.

6. A Where to Find Me page (this is for nonfiction authors). If you write nonfiction, then platform means everything. Speaking and doing radio appearances are great ways to get your name out there as you establish yourself as an expert. On your website, keep an updated schedule of where you'll be. This way those who want to connect with you in person will get that chance. Plus, you never know when an agent or editor may stop by during your talk.

Content Is King – Published Authors

This section builds on everything presented in the previous section that was tailored to unpublished authors, but it takes those points a few steps further to really make sure that as a published author you get the most out of your website. **As you work to either spruce up your existing site or piece**

together something new, add these thoughts to your must-do list:

1. Develop a tagline. I realize most authors get hung up on taglines, so let's spend some time to demystify them. **First of all, they don't need to be *Mad Men*-quality.** They just need to communicate what you write so that visitors who enjoy reading what you write will poke around a bit more.

The problem that most face when developing their taglines is they haven't really identified WHAT it is they want to write. They may dabble in three separate genres at once, but what they don't understand is that careers are started by focusing on ONE of those areas. My advice is to look at whatever series or project you're currently working on and/or most excited about and make that your "thing." (You can always change your tagline after your career picks up and you move on to other themes within that specific genre.)

If you're writing a romantic comedy set in Texas, your tagline could be "Emma Cotes—Texas-Sized Romantic Comedies." Or if you write sword and sorcery fantasy, your tagline could be "Jason Fitzpatrick—Putting Dragons Back in Fantasy Since 2005." Or it could be as simple as "Jason Fitzpatrick—Sword and Sorcery Fantasy." It doesn't have to impress. It just needs to attract the right reader.

But remember, the more specific, the better. Most authors will try to make their taglines all artsy and end up with something that just doesn't make sense. Stick to what's obvious. Your readers will appreciate it.

2. Include recent photos. I've already harped on this, but it's worth mentioning again. There's a tendency among publishing professionals to use photos that were taken twenty years ago when they were thin and "attractive," but people want and need to see the present-day you. And it must be in high quality, not some cropped shot that your niece took when you were at the park.

3. Showcase your books. Whether on your About page or on a separate page, entitled "Books" (no need to come up with anything creative), you should display the covers and back cover blurbs for your books along with links to buy them on Amazon and Barnes & Noble.

4. Get busy. There's nothing worse than an author website that the author doesn't actually do anything with. Whether on Facebook, your blog, or your website, be sure to highlight your comings and goings as an author. If you're attending conferences, announce it beforehand. Same goes for any signings, readings, or appearances you may make in-store or on the radio or web.

Zombie Sites

I'm a firm believer that the main reason e-book authors have taken off without the help of publishing houses is that they're active. They make marketing a full-time job and cherish each and every fan interaction. Their sites are constantly being updated, and they make a point to become their readers' friends.

On the other side of the fence sit a bunch of traditionally published authors—authors who spend all of their time writing for the next deadline and don't have time to update their websites or respond to blog comments. They may not even have time to blog at all! Their websites end up looking like zombie sites—places where outdated information exists. Fans may find contact information there, but they're left to wonder whether an e-mail or letter would even get read. These abandoned, unkempt sites end up as zombies. They are neither living nor dead, and they quickly suck the life out of your career. (Okay, that was a bit over the top, but stay with me here.)

Taking the steps toward developing or updating your website shouldn't be something you feel pressured into doing by any means, but any successful author will tell you that interacting with fans should be something you *want* to do.

Are you ready to bridge the gap and become friends with your readers? Are you ready to structure your writing, your life, and your business so that your fans become more of a priority?

I hope so! I hope you're ready to put your fans first and make them a priority. As a result, you'll be making your *career* a priority.

All authors should develop this aggressive mentality if they want to make it in today's market. Take George R. R. Martin, for example. The guy has a major best selling series, an HBO television series, a full conference circuit, and still takes the time to sign books that are mailed to him. Now *that's* reader service!

(If you really are the next great American novelist, you still don't get a pass on this pep talk. Honestly, you'll probably become an invalid at some point à la J. D. Salinger, Harper Lee, and Emily Dickinson, and in that type of situation your fans could very well be what save you from insanity.)

5
BLOGS

Blogging is the easiest way for any author to get his or her feet wet when it comes to building a platform. It has a free-form approach, meaning you can be as long-winded as you like, and free blogging services (available from blogspot.com, wordpress.com, and more) make it fairly easy to pick up on. They even come with tutorials. It's a win-win.

But blogging doesn't come without its share of hurdles.

There are approximately 150+ million blogs. That's 150+ million people screaming for attention. For your blog to rise out of this noisy mess, it needs to be really good. And for it to result in a salable platform, let's just say it needs to be near perfect.

How to Get Started

As mentioned above, there are a number of blogging sites where you can set everything up for free. If you're a complete newbie, I recommend using Blogger. If you're familiar with websites and what goes into building and maintaining them, then WordPress is a great option.

Before you get started, you'll need to think through a number of things:

1. What is your blog's GOAL? You'll find me asking this quite frequently throughout this little book. Without a goal, your efforts will quickly morph into something chaotic and useless. Ask yourself what you want your blog to do. Entertain readers? Offer information? Support your book? Support your career?

2. What is your blog's NAME? Yes, your blog will need a name—something catchy and memorable. My personal blog is called *Swedish Pankakes*. (Yes, the misspelling is intentional.) It chronicles my personal life. A blog name can be as simple as *Ramblings from a Romance Author* or even *The Parenting Zone*. Be creative, but be clear.

3. What is your blog's URL? You will need to create a URL when you sign up for your blog. This usually looks something like www.YourNameHere.wordpress.com. You want that first part of your blog's name to be easy to remember. This is why naming your blog is such an important part of the process. You don't want to call your blog *Mary's Musings* and then end up with a URL that's www.MaryJonesPhilly.blogspot.com.

It should be noted that you'll be given the option of purchasing a domain name that doesn't include the blogger.com or wordpress.com endings. Be thinking if this is something you want to do, but also be intentional about what you choose for a domain. Domains rank high with searchability. Be sure to have strong keywords in your domain—words that tend to be searched often on Google and other search engines.

4. What is your blog's DESIGN? You want to think through your colors and any design themes that may be present in your blog. It may be worthwhile to hire a designer to put together a masthead or banner for you (college kids will do this inexpensively) and then go off of that design. You also want to make sure that your design reflects your goal. If your goal is to encourage others through your words and writing, you don't want a dark, eerie website. You want a relaxing place where readers can kick back and relax.

5. What is your blog's LAYOUT? When signing up for your free blog, you will be presented with a number of layouts and templates. Although you'll be able to adjust this at any time, it's a good idea to go into things with an understanding of how you want your blog organized. And, if you're at a total loss, it's always safe to choose an option that has a simple left- or right-hand navigation.

Crafting Perfect Posts

The reason there are 150+ million blogs is because everyone has something to say (or at least they think they do). Of those 150+ million blogs, 149.9 million are written poorly. And the basic rule of writing is that you don't get anywhere with a poorly written blog or manuscript, right?

There are a ton of books on blogging. Each will probably offer you more information than what I'm about to present, and they may even do so in a more entertaining fashion—bells, confetti, and joke after joke after joke. But I've been blogging for awhile now, and I've also read a lot of equally great and bad blogs. In an effort to condense everything into a digestible sub-section, I've identified a few of the many rules of blogging. These are the rules I see broken, mangled, and abused most often. And these are the rules that will quickly make your blog a zillion times better (or thereabouts) should you uphold them.

Five Important and Essential Rules of Blogging

1. Stick to the goal. I can't stress it enough. Your blog absolutely must have a goal. What do you want your blog to accomplish? Structure your posts around that goal.

Do you want to promote yourself as an author/speaker/expert? Do you want to promote your book? Do you want to connect with fans? Do you want to offer an online experience that ties in with your book? These are important questions, and without answering them, your blog will turn into a mush of information.

For example, many in the publishing industry have come to know and love Chip MacGregor's blog (chipmacgregor.com). He provides valuable information on the industry and is a huge help to writers. But what would happen if Chip suddenly started blogging about the Oregon Ducks? He certainly loves them enough to do so, and those who know him know he isn't shy about his affections. What if every other post was a recap of their games and dealings? And then what if he shifted gears with his blog on the weekends and talked all about dancing? (Yes, Chip dances.) What would happen then?

I'll tell you what would happen: he'd start to lose readers. Sure, he'd gain a few who are interested in the Ducks and dancing, but all of the readers who rely on his blog for publishing insight would soon find other places to go. The bottom line is that he wouldn't be hitting his target market anymore. He'd instead be hitting a niche market interested in publishing, the Oregon Ducks, *and* dancing. Not exactly a best-seller-sized readership.

When your blog lacks a clear, singular goal, you will either lose readers that you'd otherwise want to keep, or gain ones who aren't going to contribute to your success in publishing. It's as simple as that.

2. Treat each post like a story with a beginning, middle, and end. It's a common mistake for bloggers to cram multiple themes/points/declarations in each blog post. What you end up with is a smorgasbord of personal opinions and experiences, and readers are left to wade through it all and extract what they want.

A good example of this happens during election season. Bloggers are often eager to share their political views, but their posts can turn into a tirade of what they love and hate about the current administration. On and on they jump from one thing to another, covering gay marriage, taxes, our nation's debt, immigration, and more until the reader's head is spinning and he or she doesn't know how to reply. I mean, who has ever had a good response to a sudden soapbox moment? No one. So, the result is readers either feel alienated or they choose to pick a fight, and neither of those options are appealing.

This is why each blog post, no matter the topic, should be treated like a book. It should have a beginning, in which it teases the reader or introduces the topic; a middle, in which it provides additional information; and an ending, in which it hits it all home and brings it together.

A good example of this is the January 15, 2010 post on my personal blog. Here it is:

EXPERIMENTING WITH SIZE 8

Tomorrow I find out if it's possible for a person to go on living without breathing for, say, six hours. In anticipation for this big event I have:

1) Worked out less
2) Eaten more
3) Blogged less
4) Worked more
5) Worried way more

I expect to go into a state of shock approximately one hour into the study. By hour two, I will begin to feel dizzy, accompanied by possible waves of nausea, neurosis and psychosis. By hour two and a half, I will lose all feeling in my feet and hands. This will slowly spread to my legs and arms and by hour four, I will, unbeknownst to those around me, move in and out of consciousness. At a quarter past hour four I will enter a preliminary stage of nirvana, and by hour five I will be frolicking in fields of wildflowers and dancing with sea lions. Only to come back to reality once hour six hits and my dress is unzipped.

Yes. Tomorrow is Ashlee's wedding, and my dress is way way way too tight.

It's a humor post, but notice how the opening line presents the subject matter in a way that is both intriguing and funny. The next few paragraphs offer supportive information, building on the subject matter without fully disclosing what the heck I'm talking about. Then the final paragraph brings it all home for an ending that (I'm hoping) is both enlightening and laugh-out-loud funny. *Note: My blog is NOT a professional blog. It's simply something that I do for me, so it doesn't follow many of these guidelines.*

To once again use our election season blog post as an example, the author would see a much better response if he or she were to choose one of those topics and craft a post that is entertaining, enlightening, and thought-provoking (as opposed to the GRRRR, I HATE THE WORLD vibe that tends to go hand in hand with political posts).

I must say that if you're pursuing nonfiction publication, your blog post endings should have a clear takeaway—something that the reader learns or can use and rewards them for reading. This will make you look like an expert who is able to help. For example, if you want to be an expert on stress management, your blog posts should leave readers with a stress-relief tip, method, or truth.

3. Keep it casual. There's this tendency to treat blogging as you would an essay—proper grammar, no contractions, complete sentences. But that's the very mindset that will kill your blog. Think of it more as a conversation with friends. Throw grammar rules to the wind and leave properly formatted sentences to your high school English teacher. Trust me, you'll get a lot more readers this way.

4. Don't forget voice! Your author voice is one of the most effective weapons you have in making your blog a success, yet you'd be surprised how many authors don't incorporate it into their blogging. Your blog is an advertisement for your books. What better way to prove you're a great writer than to have a strong, compelling blogging voice?

For the record, your blogging voice can vary vastly from your novel-writing voice. Mine does. People read my blog posts and think I'm planning to be the next David Sedaris. But I have no desire to write entire books of memoir or sarcastic, cheap-witted prose. (Not that David Sedaris writes cheapwittedly. That's just how I view my own nonfiction style. In fact, I'm surprised you've made it this far into this book!) Instead, I want to write women's speculative fiction. Needless to say, my fiction voice is exponentially different than my blogging voice, yet many times my blogging voice has caused people to become intrigued with the fiction that I write for fun.

5. Avoid the "daily diary" syndrome. This is probably the biggest problem for those 149.9 million bloggers who can't seem to get traction, and it can be summed up in one sentence: no one cares what you had for dinner.

There's this tendency to treat a blog like a journal where you archive your day's events. But no one cares that you went to the grocery store after picking up Travis from football practice. And no one cares that you found ground beef on sale for two dollars a pound.

If you're blogging about your personal life (this goes back to rule #1), avoid the tendency to rehash all of your day's events. Pick *one* event, and form a blog post around it. Give it a beginning, middle and end, and your blog will leave readers wanting more.

I hate to be pointing you to my personal blog, since it's not a shining example of perfection, but if you look at that post again, you'll see that I wrote it the day before my best friend's wedding. I had a million topics to choose from. I could have written about her dress or the decor or the strange guy I had to walk with down the aisle. I could have written about how I barely got off work in time to be there or how I was wearing shoes with million-inch heels. But instead of cramming all that juicy (and sometimes entertaining) information into a never-ending post, I selected one thing that I felt encapsulated the experience. And, truth be told, that blog post almost landed me a major marketing job at a university.

Building a Following
Once you've mastered (and I mean MASTERED) blog writing,

then you can focus on drawing readers to your blog.

What? You mean I don't just sit back and wait for them to come to me?

You can, but it will take you years and years to develop an even remotely impressive following. If you want to expedite the process, this section is for you.

The Technical Approach

There are some techie things you can do to make your blog more searchable on sites like Google and Bing. The more searchable it is, the more likely people will stumble across it. This is a great technique for nonfiction bloggers, because you're typically offering answers or solutions to problems that people have. For example, let's say you're an expert on child psychology. Some frantic parent goes to Google and types in something like "how to get my teen to talk to me." You'd want your site to show up in the search results, wouldn't you?

Follow these steps and that just might happen.

1. Title it right. Google is structured so that the title of your blog post helps determine its position within searches. The more searchable terms/keywords that a title has, the more likely it is to be pulled up in a search result. Confused?

Most search engines work like this: When people conduct an online search, the search engine, in its infinite wisdom, pulls out what it deems to be the keywords of that search. You can throw an entire sentence at it, and it will pull out the proper nouns, nouns, and possibly verbs. It then moves across the Internet to find a match for those terms, and page titles weigh heavily in this search. This is why it's key to avoid vague blog post titles, such as "Introducing My New Book!" and "Happy to Be Home!" These will get you nowhere because the words within them are overused and vague. They aren't specific enough. Still confused? Stay with me here.

Let's say you do a blog post on your next book, which is about a cowboy winning the heart of a school teacher. You at first want to name the post "My Next Book!" but realize that would be Google suicide because the odds of your post coming up when someone searches for "book" are like a zillion to one. No one searches for "my next book" or even "my book" or "next book."

So, you do a bit of research and figure out that search terms like "cowboy" and "modern cowboy" and "cowboy bachelors" are all strong. Then consider what you would type into Google if you were interested in modern cowboys and romance.

You develop a blog post entitled "5 Ways to Attract a Modern Day Cowboy." This will draw readers who are interested in cowboys, romance, and potentially your book. This title is also much more searchable than your original one because it's packed full of appropriately grouped search terms that are going to attract the perfect reader. Plus, numbered posts rock ("5 Ways to…," "10 Secrets of…," etc.). These are hugely popular and will ensure that if people stumble across your post on Google, they'll actually click it.

2. Link to other sites. Another way to increase SEO (search engine optimization) is to link to other sites within your post. It's ideal when those sites then link back to you, but it's not always feasible.

For those of you totally new to blogging, a link is a live chunk of text (usually appears in blue or underlined), and when you click on it, it takes you to a new web page.

When adding these hyperlinks to your blog post, you simply copy the URL that you want to link to, highlight the text in your blog post that you want to hold the link, and then apply the link using the fancy hyperlink button in your blogging toolbar.

Whatever you do, avoid anchoring the link to the word "here."

For example, "Check out our agency website here."

This is bad. Just as search engines heavily weigh page titles, they also weigh words that are the anchors for hyperlinks. They count them toward that page's searchability. The word "here" isn't a good search term because it could mean anything and be associated with numerous searches. I could use the word "here" when searching for "here vs. hear" or "right here right now lyrics." In other words, there would be so many search results that would appear *before* our MacGregor Literary page would pop up.

Instead, it's best to anchor the link to key search terms that are associated with the destination link. By doing this, your link will be better matched with online searches since the search engine can easily verify that you know what you're talking about within your blog post.

Here's an example of a link done right: "Check out the MacGregor Literary agency website."

3. Spread the word. One of the easiest ways to spread the word about your blog is to share links to it through your social media and info-sharing sites, such as Facebook, Twitter, Pinterest, StumbleUpon, Digg, Reddit, etc. This involves adding a "Share This" or "Add This" widget or even little social media buttons to the end of each blog post. This is something that is set up on the back end of your site, and it may involve tweaking the HTML coding. If you're unsure how to do that, find someone who can either show you how or do it for you.

You should make a point to put your posts and links to your blog on Google+ as much as possible. You see, Google loves Google+ because they're kind of related. One smart thing to do is to get all of your friends who have Google accounts to share your posts on Google+. This will help Google favor your site a bit more when it's determining what kinds of search results to offer. (Google+ is Google's version of Facebook.)

Keep in mind, however, that readers are lazy. If they get used to finding your blog through Twitter or Facebook or any other social media site, they're going to rely on you to share those links in those same spots every time. And the moment you stop sharing, they stop reading. Once you start putting your posts on any of these sites, you must be consistent. I had a few readers of my blog find me through StumbleUpon. If I forgot or was too busy to put my new posts on that site, then the readers simply would not come looking for my site. They waited patiently until I had the time to share via StumbleUpon, and *then* they'd read and get caught up.

Note: On Blogger, sharing via Google+ is as simple as clicking the "share this on Google+" button in the top toolbar. It's another reason why Blogger is ridiculously easy to use.

4. Post regularly. There's nothing more destructive than when bloggers abandon their active blogs for lengthy periods of time. Do yourself a favor and commit to a schedule that is do-able. Start by posting once per week. Post on the same day and preferably at the same time each day. This will develop a readership.

When you feel as though you can do more, expand to two posts per week. But never commit to something that you can't live up to. As a reader of multiple blogs, it gets old really fast when bloggers commit to things and then never follow through.

Let's use my column on ChipMacgregor.com as an example. I blog only once a week (every Thursday, to be exact), and my column has a solid following. And there are readers of my column who will only show up for Thursday's post. This proves that consistency is key and you really can build a following with less.

The Relational Approach

Now that you know a bunch of technical things you can do to make your blog more searchable and attractive, let's discuss what it takes to keep readers.

1. Write with your readers in mind. It may be more fun to write about yourself and your very interesting life, but just as you enjoy writing for *yourself*, readers enjoy reading for *themselves*. Blog posts that deliver on reader expectations go a long way.

2. Pose a question or discussion point at the end. A

simple "What Christmas memories do YOU have?" or "What have you found useful when house hunting?" can go a long way with making your readers feel like your real friends rather than your Internet stalkers. Now, don't overcomplicate this. There's no need for multi-layered questions or uber thought-provoking stuff. Keep it simple and inviting. Make your blog a safe place for others to interact.

3. Reply to comments. To encourage a healthy blog community, it's best to reply to as many comments as you can, even if you just thank the commenters for stopping by. This will keep readers coming back. Not only are you acknowledging their participation, but you're proving yourself to be active on your blog and interested in what each person has to say. People post comments because they want to be heard. They want attention. Give them that ear. Give them the attention they crave, and they'll be coming back for more.

4. Offer visual stimuli. Pictures, videos, and even GIFs (Google the term if you don't know what it is) are magical, little beings that keep readers reading. They offer a visual break and can make long posts feel shorter. Furthermore, try not to write in huge paragraphs, and as best you can, avoid going over 800 words. I've found that block paragraphs of 2–4 sentences are best.

Blogging as a Fiction Writer

Blogging as a fiction writer is difficult. If I were in your shoes, I'd probably choose something else with which to build my platform, like Facebook or Twitter. They're easier. Unlike nonfiction authors, fiction authors aren't really experts on anything. People don't come to them looking for answers or solutions or world peace. They don't have that clear topic to drive their blogs. They just have themselves and their imaginations. And that doesn't always make for an interesting blog experience.

How do you make blogging work when you're a fiction author who's trying to grow a platform? Here are my thoughts, and this time they *are* in a particular order:

1. Know your book's reader. While research is the best way to find your reader, you can get a rough picture of your reader through genre and theme. This goes back to Chapter One, but for the sake of this section, I'll summarize.

Genre—You can make assumptions about your reader based on what you know to be true of the genre or category in which you're writing.

EXAMPLE: If you write YA fiction, then your primary readers are teens. If you write testosterone-driven thrillers, then your readers are men in their 30s, 40s, and 50s. If you write contemporary romance, your readers are women.

Theme—Themes, elements, or hobbies that appear in your writing may also point to a certain readership.

EXAMPLE: You write contemporary romance. Great. But on top of that, you tend to pepper your stories with scrapbooking themes or characters who have taken up this specific hobby. You know that scrapbooking is typically enjoyed by a specific type of person, meaning the themes will draw a specific kind of reader. This gives you a much narrower target than just saying your readership is women. Your readership is now women who scrapbook.

2. Build your blog around your reader. Now that you know a bit about your readers, you can create a blog that is geared toward them and their interests.

EXAMPLE: You've determined that your contemporary romances appeal to women who scrapbook. Instead of blogging about your day or the stresses of writing, you decide to start a blog all about scrapbooking. You share tips, photos, and links to things that inspire others, and you quickly realize that the people who are drawn to your blog are the very people who would be interested in reading your book.

3. Follow the steps outlined in the Building a Following sections. Your keywords should be related to whatever theme you've chosen for your blog, and your post titles should appeal to your readership.

EXAMPLE: For your scrapbooking blog, you might post things like "10 Scrapbooking Trends" and comparisons on what embellishment brands you like the best and what stores you prefer: "Michaels vs. Hobby Lobby vs. Archivers." The basic idea here is if you focus your blog on scrapbooking news, trends, and tips, you'll gain a natural following. Then you can eventually mention your book without making the whole blog about your writing career.

4. Give away the goods. Develop flash fiction or chapter downloads to get your blog readers interested in your fiction. You'll come out of that experience with a number of people who are dedicated to helping you succeed.

EXAMPLE: You write a handful of scrapbooking short stories. You then announce this on your blog and get people curious. You can either post the stories as blog posts or publish them on sites like Smashwords.com, gifting them to the readers who ask. Try to be consistent with this, coming out with new material every three months or so. Eventually, you'll have some people who come to love your fiction. These are your first true fans.

5. Have a plan for migrating fans to your author sites. You don't want to develop fans of your writing only to leave them on your non-writing-related blog. Figure out a way to move them over to a more comfortable place for you to communicate your writing updates without bothering the rest of your blog readership.

EXAMPLE: You soon find that after completing steps 1–4, you've developed a good number of blog readers who have also turned into fans of your writing, but you can't turn your blog into a hub for your writing career. This is the point where you create a separate space for your writing fans to congregate, whether on Facebook, Twitter, or another blog or Tumblr site.

Pep Talk

You can do it. You can do it. You can do it. If you don't think you can do it, then feel free to walk away. But I'm telling you,

YOU'VE GOT THIS. Blogging is one of the more intuitive networking options for authors these days. It's the only place where you can truly use your voice and your craft as they were meant to be used. Think about it, determine what you can commit to, and then don't just give it a shot, but give it your all.

You can do it.

6
TWITTER

I was on a plane recently with a gentleman who found out I was an agent, and he started asking me about the industry. He had a book idea and a bunch of questions to go with it. Eventually he started asking about formatting the manuscript and design and all of that stuff.

"You don't have to worry about that," I said. "Authors have two responsibilities: deadlines and marketing. They have to get their manuscripts turned in on time and then market the heck out of their books."

And that's where the conversation took a turn.

"I didn't know authors had to be marketers," he said. "I thought they just sat in their homes and wrote and wrote and didn't talk to a soul." He laughed, of course, because this is how society sees writers.

Twenty years ago, he would have been right, but the Internet changed everything. It made the world smaller.

And Twitter is as small as it can possibly get.

A mere ten years ago, celebrities were untouchable. If you wanted to know about their lifestyles, you read the tabloids or watched the MTV show *Cribs*. If you wanted to meet them, you stalked their tour buses or started working out in LA gyms. Or you'd stand outside of the MTV studios in Time Square or set up camp in LAX, studying the faces of passersby. But even these strategies would fail. Meeting a celebrity was an occurrence left to chance.

But these days it's as easy as sending a text message.

I follow Zach Braff on Twitter. He's an actor/director/writer, most well-known for his work on the TV show *Scrubs* and the movies *Garden State* and *Oz the Great and Powerful*. He's a decent-sized celebrity, but on Twitter, he's just a regular guy. He dispels tabloid rumors before they even start, shares photos of his happenings, and tells jokes. He lets his hundreds of thousands of fans in on his everyday life, and he repays their support and love by interacting with them. He responds to their questions and laughs at their jokes. He's involved.

Literary agents are following suit. The stories of old tell how we were untouchable and impossible to reach. They tell how conferences were the only places where people could prove that we did exist. But not anymore. In the past year, I heard a handful of stories from writers who claimed that Twitter was what opened the door to them landing their agents. Not only that, but we have the #askagent hashtag and Sara Megibow's brilliant #10QueriesIn10Tweets along with other great strategies that agents are putting forward to be visible online.

Agents—stuffy, scary, angry, mean agents—are on Twitter.

Here's the bottom line: If I can get Zach Braff or Ashton Kutcher or Taylor Swift or Barack Obama or Donald Maass or some other big-time, hotshot to respond to my tweets, shouldn't I be able to get my favorite author to do the same? And at the very least, shouldn't mid-list and new authors be *more* available on Twitter than high-profile actors and musicians and agents?

If the Internet made the world smaller, then Twitter has turned everyone into next-door neighbors. And as authors, writers, and future celebrities, it's your job to be available to your fans.

While you're mulling that over, go set up a Twitter account and follow your favorite celebrity. Then tell me if you don't feel more connected to him or her in a warm, fuzzy way.

How to Get Started

If you're unfamiliar with Twitter, the best thing to do is create an account, poke around, and then just sit back and watch it for a month or two. See how people use it, and notice what works and what doesn't. Twitter is so very different from other social media sites that it just takes some getting used to. Allow yourself that time. You'll catch on, and quickly realize that Tweets are nothing more than fancy Internet text messages.

How to Write Great Tweets

To write well for Twitter, you really need to change your mindset. I've seen novelists, who are used to writing 100,000+ word manuscripts, balk when it comes to Tweeting, and I've seen successful business types equally fail when they take the hard sell approach. Twitter isn't a place for you to flaunt your knowledge of the English language or refine your author voice. It's not a place where constantly telling people to buy your book or visit your website will work either. Twitter takes a bit more finesse, a bit more thought, and a lot more of a marketing or sales-focused mindset.

Twitter restricts the number of characters used in each Tweet to 140. If you're curious what that looks like, note this paragraph. Yep, 140.

It may seem like a lot to work with at first, but once you add any @ mentions or links or hashtags, it can get crowded fast. It's this very crowdedness that hinders authors from being successful with their Tweets.

But if you can learn to write compelling, actionable copy for Twitter, you can write just about anything.

Just like any other social media channel, the basic rule to a great Twitter account is to have a goal. Do you want to sell books? Generate interest in your website or blog? Position yourself as an expert on a topic? Have fun with readers? A clear goal will guide each and every Tweet, preventing you from flooding your readers with conflicting information. With a goal, you'll be sure to attract the very readers that care about the Tweets you throw at them. And *that* is where the Twitter magic happens.

But how do you construct compelling copy in 140 characters? I'm glad you asked.

The Three Components of a Great Tweet

1. It has a CALL TO ACTION. The Tweet must either provide worthwhile information or ask the reader to DO something. For example, if you're going to be speaking in the Chicago area, you could Tweet about it, encouraging Chicagoans to come out and see you. Or you could ask readers to check out your speaking schedule (include a link) to see when you'll be in their area. The ideal strategy would be to do both: share your speaking schedule link when you've got your summer tour nailed down, and then Tweet about each city a day or so before you arrive.

Sample Tweet: Excited to b doing a reading @ Anderson's in Naperville @7pm! Come see me if u can. I'd love to meet up after it's over <link here>

2. It has a HOOK. The Tweet must grab the reader's attention. Many Twitter users follow hundreds if not thousands of people, and that's a lot of competition. Get your Tweets to stand out by always ensuring they draw the reader in. Avoid lots of hard sell Tweets (e.g., *Buy my book!*). This is where creativity is a must.

3. It has LINKS and/or HASHTAGS. A great Tweet will direct your readers to places where they can get more information.

Linking to photos is a great way to connect with your readers through those less sales-related Tweets.

Sample Tweet: Thanks to everyone who came out to hear me speak at the #ChicagoPublicLibrary It was awesome! <link to photo of speaker with fans>

Linking to a website is a great way to provide extra information and a harder sell without coming across too strong.

Sample Tweet: Thanks to everyone who came out tonight! Next up, Indianapolis <link to speaking schedule on website>

NOTE: Twitter will automatically shorten your links to 20 characters, leaving you with 120 to work with.

Hashtags and Links and Images! Oh My!

One of the first things you'll notice about Twitter is the heavy use of hashtags (the things that start with a #), links, and pictures. Most Tweets contain at least one of these items, and that's because these are the things that generate interest, reach new followers, and keep Twitter interesting.

Hashtags look like this: #creativewriting #allIwantforChristmas. They are a hash sign, followed by a string of words or an acronym that uses no punctuation or spaces. You can create your own hashtags simply by Tweeting them. Hashtags are not owned or registered. They are free to use, create, and reuse.

Essentially, a hashtag is a way to categorize your Tweet. It's nothing more than a callout that allows others with similar interests to find you if they so choose.

For example, people who were interested in the 2012 presidential debates used the hashtag #debate2012 to categorize their appropriate Tweets and make sure that they went into the big pool of people talking about the debates. Those who really wanted to follow what others were saying about the debates would simply monitor the #debate2012 hashtag. (Monitoring a hashtag is as simple as typing it into Twitter's search bar and checking the results. They stream live, meaning you don't have to refresh your browser.)

Jumping on a trending hashtag will broaden your readership, because there will already be tons of people out there also talking about and watching that specific hashtag.

How to Find the Right Hashtags

Like I said above, hashtags are not owned and therefore cannot be stolen. They're free for the taking and using. But how do you know which hashtags are being used the most? That's what you want, right? You want the biggest bang for your buck, and you don't have time to be Tweeting never-used hashtags if there are better ones out there with built-in followings.

Three ways to find hashtags:
1. Ask Google. I do this all the time. If I want to share something on Twitter that I feel is really important, I'll do a Google search that helps me see what hashtags my intended audience uses most. My search typically looks like "top hashtags for authors" or "top hashtags for bloggers" or "top hashtags for dog lovers." (Yes, I Tweet about my dog A LOT.) If you're Tweeting about your book, you may want to look up the top hashtags for your genre or even the themes presented in your book (primarily for nonfiction authors), such as personal finance, parenting, and, to come full circle, even scrapbooking.

2. Ask Twitter. Somewhat akin to throwing darts at a dartboard while blindfolded, this is the method in which you invent your own hashtags and then plug them into Twitter (or a service like Topsy.com) to see how frequently they're used. If you come away with results that show the hashtag being used multiple times every day, it's a pretty good hashtag. Anything less than that, and you have to weigh whether it's worth it or not. In some instances it just might be.

3. Follow the strongest hashtags. Services such as Tweetdeck or Hootsuite allow users to keep an eye on hashtags and keywords of their choice. If you're consistent about reviewing what these sites pull for you, you'll probably discover some new hashtags that appeal to your target audience. Often users will Tweet with more than one hashtag, meaning there is plenty of room for you to spot hashtag trends and jump on them.

What Does a Great Tweet Look Like?

They aren't always grammatically pretty, and the limited character count oftentimes has you talking like a texting teenager. But it's time to cast any word-related snobbiness aside. Great Tweets are ugly, yet effective. Here are some I put together:

Like Romeo & Juliet? LOVE #vampires? Check out my new book TWILIGHT <linkhere> #YAparanormal—*This Tweet works because it gets the reader answering "yes" to each of the preliminary questions. They're already thinking "yes" when they come to the pitch. It's a bit of a hard sell, but it works. Readers feel comfortable with hard sells that are well thought out.*

What happens when a #serialkiller runs a hotel at the world fair? I wondered the same thing <link to blog post on book idea here> #nonfiction—*This Tweet uses the book's one-liner for a HOOK, and then it moves readers to a harmless post that will hopefully pique interest and result in sales, or at the very least awareness.*

At B&N 2nite @ 7:30p in Rosemont. Get a #freebook when u upload a pic of us. Details <linkhere> #fiction #bookgiveaway—*This Tweet is a great example of using Twitter to promote. Plus, it will encourage additional buzz when readers accept the challenge and start uploading their pictures with the author. The pictures will reach potential readers outside of the author's original circle, thus generating more awareness.*

Thing to love #4: dress blues. Find 1000 more things to love <linkhere> #militarylife #militaryspouse —*This Tweet uses a teaser from the book,* 1001 Things to Love About Military Life *to generate interest.*

Building a Following

Twitter is a lot more relational than its 140-character limit would lead you to believe. Like I said, I've heard of authors finding agents, new readers, and even publishers through their Tweets. But *how* does this happen? How do you take a short, insignificant Tweet and turn it into an opportunity?

The answer is you don't. Instead, you build rapport over time, slowly wooing your targets and ultimately winning them over.

So, like everything else in this book, here are a handful of ideas for finding and wooing new readers:

The Search and Find Method. Hashtags, keywords, and terms are all searchable on Twitter. This makes it rather easy to find other Tweeters who are interested in either what you write or the genre you write in. Let me explain...

Pretend you're a fantasy author. Punch in "epic fantasy" and you'll get all of the latest Tweets containing that phrase. Each Tweet is an opportunity. It represents a real person who probably loves the fantasy genre. But the term "epic fantasy" isn't a good conversation starter. So, you type in "Feast for Crows," which is one of the latest George R. R. Martin novels. Again, Twitter kicks back results, but this time you have something to talk about—Martin. Instead of cold-calling these potential followers, you woo them.

The Gimmick Method. Oh, this sounds *so* lame, but it's actually one of the more clever tactics (and it happens to work best for nonfiction authors). Here's the gist...

Think of something that you're good at—something you have to offer that others desire. Then give away the goods. A good example of this comes from the #AskAgent hashtag. Agents all over use this hashtag when they plan to answer questions from writers via Twitter. They advertise the date and time that they plan to be available, and then they simply wait for the questions to roll in, using the #AskAgent hashtag. It's a great way for an agent to grow his or her following and come across as an expert.

The same type of method could be achieved by nearly every type of expert. Simply create an #AskRelationshipDoc or #AskChildShrink or #AskPastorDave hashtag, advertise a date and time when you'll be available, and then actually BE available and interactive during that said time. You're bound to find a chunk of potential followers because you're giving away advice for free, and who doesn't want advice?

The LiveTweet Method. I've seen authors who have a steady Twitter following do live Tweeting during a fan-favorite television show (*Downton Abbey* for the regency or historical author, *The Walking Dead* or *True Blood* for the paranormal author, etc.). All they do is create a hashtag by which other participants may follow the conversation. Then they Tweet their thoughts during the show and also respond to other people's thoughts. Sounds messy, and it probably would be for someone new to Twitter. But this method hits a need with some fiction fans who want to feel close to their favorite authors.

The Conversational Method. If slow and steady wins the race, then this is the gold medal option for creating a following on Twitter. This method involves being highly active on Twitter and very present in your followers' Tweet streams. It means reTweeting and replying to people you don't know. It means mentioning others in your Tweets as much as possible and maybe even offering up the occasional direct message. In essence, this is the method that requires you to live on Twitter and treat your followers just as you would treat your e-mail inbox or your Facebook profile. Everyone gets responses from you, and everyone gets acknowledged.

The Stalker Method. There's something to be said for finding potential followers on Twitter and then going the extra mile. Yep, you heard me. I'm talking about visiting blogs. If you leave a few comments on someone's blog and then connect with them via Twitter, they're likely to follow you or at least pay some sort of attention to your Tweets.

So, there you have it—some basic ideas on how to gain a following through Twitter (aside from the typical method of begging).

7
FACEBOOK

Using Facebook to promote yourself as an author seems like a no-brainer. After all, *everyone's* doing it. You should too, right? Well…

I think I speak for all of us when I say that I roll my eyes, groan loudly, and hit "Delete" when faced with "Like" requests from pages like Kaufmann Realty or Investors' Insurance or—and I'm not making this one up—the Cardinal Fitness mascot. It's not that I don't like those companies; it's just that they haven't answered the million dollar question…

What's in it for me?

While Facebook is highly commercialized, it's still a very personal experience. It's a representation of who you are. And while you may not know every person on your friends list, you certainly want to give them the chance to know you. So, you dig around for only the best timeline cover photo. You painstakingly rearrange your activity so that only the most impressive things show up. You carefully select music, movies, and hobbies that reflect who you are.

And as for "Likes," you only "Like" things that reflect your personality. Your style.

Unless! Unless they offer something in return that is simply irresistible.

Cardy the Cardinal had nothing to offer me—no coupons for free spin cycle classes, no updates on dead times at the gym. I couldn't even find updated information on local running events or gym hours. There was nothing in it for me. And since I had no connection with Cardy the Cardinal other than the fact that I was a member of his gym, I deleted the request.

This, my friends, is an example of the main pitfall of using Facebook to promote yourself as an author. You assume that since you're among family and friends and readers, they'll all want to be part of your writing experience. But who wants to "Like" a page only to be updated every time the author writes a thousand words in one hour? Who wants to hear about rejections and NaNoWriMo and "OMG I just figured out why my protag is the way she is!!!"?

The answer is *other writers*. Other writers want to hear about this stuff. They want to talk about it and analyze it and gush over it again and again. But actual fans don't care.

Writing for Writers vs. Writing for Readers

The greatest issue that I see with authors using Facebook to promote themselves is that they focus it in a way that it targets *other writers* when it should be targeting *readers*.

Other writers don't buy your books. They don't come to your events and sit and listen at your readings. Why? Because they're busy with their own books and their own events. And that little thing called jealousy can sometimes get in the way, too.

But readers? Readers will support you, love you, and tout your books. Readers are the ones writers should target with all of their social media efforts, not just their Facebook groups and pages. To do that successfully, writers need to provide a takeaway that is irresistible (but more on that later).

How to Get Started

First things first, you need a personal profile. If you don't have one of these, go to Facebook and set one up. Your profile is what you'll use to interact with friends and family and maintain some sort of personal life. But on top of this, you'll need a professional page.

Now, to be super clear for the all the Facebook newbies, a professional page is a page where users must "Like" it in order to join. If you'd like to see my agent page, you can check it out at facebook.com/AgentAmandaLuedeke. A *personal profile* is where people send you friend requests if they want to link up with you.

Professional Page vs. Personal Profile

Facebook is one of those places where you can quickly turn into an annoying friend. Take me for instance…

I joined Facebook way back in 2005. My reason for joining was so that I could stay in touch with my college friends after graduation (that, and I got pressured into it). So, for years I'd used Facebook primarily to strengthen friendships, stay in touch with family, and stalk the occasional random person.

When I became an agent, things changed. I quickly realized that people would want to connect with me online. (Well, I didn't realize this so much as I was *shown* it when I suddenly got a bunch of friend requests from people I didn't know.) While some authors really struggle with the idea of "friending" those they don't personally know, that sort of thing doesn't bother me. I was happy to friend strangers, and I didn't mind when they commented on my updates and photos and such.

However, the real issue for me came when I knew I needed to provide some sort of insight into my career. After all, these individuals were connecting with me online because I was an *agent*, and not because we were besties or went to the same high school or had anything in common whatsoever.

Now, could I simply start posting about my agenting life? Sure. BUT! I knew that doing so would really annoy my *real* friends.

Many authors face this same predicament. They end up pooling all of their online connections together in one spot—friends, family, readers, fans, industry professionals. With so many crammed into the same space, it gets difficult to meet their varying needs without making a few of them mad.

This is why the first rule of using Facebook for both private and professional use is that you must, must, must separate the two. Keep a personal profile for yourself and then put together a professional page for your career-self. Sure, you can link from your personal profile to your professional page now and then or share really exciting things on your personal page, but the goal here is to give Uncle Ed the option to follow your career if he so chooses. Let *him* decide. He's much less likely to block or become annoyed with you this way.

Setting Up a Professional Page

If you already have a Facebook profile, setting up a professional page is really as simple as going to any professional Facebook page and clicking on the "Create Page" button on the right.

From there, you'll be guided through the process quite seamlessly. However, **there are some things you may want to think through beforehand**:

1. Who is my target audience and what is my goal? Do you want to entice potential readers of your Career Advice Book by offering stats, tips, and links all pertaining to careers? Do you want to connect with current readers by keeping them in the loop? Do you want to energize your biggest fans by arming them with what they need to tell others about you and your books? As you can see, it's worth thinking this through, because your page's goal will affect how you use it and what information you place on it.

2. What is an appropriate title for my page? I went with "Amanda Luedeke—Literary Agent," but you may want to simply go with "Bill Smith—Thriller Author" or "The KC Ayers Fan Club" or "Daily Career Tips."

3. What information should I provide? You're going to have a lot of space on your About page to fill with info. Don't dial it in and simply answer Facebook's prompts. Be intentional. If you want your travel schedule or book release dates more readily available for the reader, then drop those in. Don't feel you have to provide your personal information or personal interests just because Facebook asks for those things. Be selective with the information you provide and make sure it gives the reader something of value.

4. What is the takeaway? Why would anyone "Like" my page? What's in it for them? These are the most important questions you can ask. And it all has to do with catering to your audience—knowing what they want and need. Will they get jazzed over author and genre news? Sneak peeks into new material? Daily how-to tips? Whatever you choose, knowing what's going to get your followers excited is key.

Succeeding with Facebook

Okay, so you have your Facebook page in place and you're ready to go. Now what? How do you foster a healthy Facebook community long term? Here's a collection of ideas. The more you can put into practice, the better, but understand that it may take some time to get the hang of things. Allow yourself some flex time, and don't be disheartened if things are slow-going at first. (And as always, you'll probably come up with many more great ideas, but hopefully these get the ball rolling.)

10 Tips for a Thriving Facebook Author Community

1. Focus your audience. This is primarily for authors who write to multiple audiences. You want to have an outlet for each of those audiences. Those who read your teen fantasy series aren't going to want to hear or talk about your adult cozy mystery series. Be careful with assuming that a fan is a fan no matter what you write. That's not always true. Keep your genres separated as best you can unless they really do cross over.

2. Pay attention to design and usability. Despite its fill-in-the-blank templates, Facebook shouldn't be overlooked as a space that needs some TLC. Take the effort and (potentially) money needed to have a really great design put together. The obvious place for this design is where the cover photo sits, but there are other spots that can be improved as well. Pay attention to everything—from customizing what is most visible on your page's top navigation (the place where it says "Photos," "Events," etc.) to adding apps that will enhance the user experience.

Take author Ted Dekker's page, for example. He's included e-mail updates and event listings in his Facebook page's top navigation. Charlaine Harris is another great example (even though some elements are a bit lackluster). She's promoting signed copies of her book on her Facebook page (as of February 2013)! And what's even better is she's driving customers to retailers. That's a win-win.

Spend time on Facebook pages such as these to get the lay of the land and maybe even some ideas of your own. *Tip: Don't discount researching product pages from your favorite brands. Usually, big name companies do things right when it comes to social media.*

3. Take advantage of Facebook's ease of use. Facebook isn't just about updating your status anymore. You can post videos, pictures, sound bites, links, blog posts, and more onto your Facebook page. Use most or all of these to keep your page fresh and visually appealing. Plus, you never know when some fans will react better to a video than a lengthy post.

4. Post regularly. Don't let the page die. Keep it populated by trying to post 3–5 things per week. Or, at the very least, be consistent. (If you begin by posting daily and then disappear for a few weeks, it won't provide the ideal user experience.) Being present on your page is essential, because Facebook is structured to highlight popular stories that it thinks users care about. To stay at the top of your followers' news feeds, be present in the space, post content that users care about (not always updates on how your dog or cat is doing), and be careful to post at times of the day when Facebook's traffic is a bit slower. This will mean that your post won't compete with other posts and it will have a better chance of being seen, which means it will have a better chance of being "Liked" or commented on and a better chance of staying high on your followers' news feeds.

5. Visit with fans. This is another weird Facebook occurrence, but I've noticed that when I interact with a friend, his or her updates tend to be more visible in my news feed and vice versa. I believe this can also apply to some extent to pages. Spending time to visit with your fans (click around on their profiles, mention them in posts, respond to their comments, etc.) will result in better visibility on their news feeds, and it will get them coming back for more. It also makes them feel pretty special.

6. Avoid talking about yourself. If you turn the page into a news feed about your kids or dog or family or job, you'll quickly sink the ship. Avoid talking about *you* (unless you really are that epic of a celebrity), and instead focus the conversation on fans. What interests them? What affects them? What do *they* want to talk about? (And for nonfiction authors, what do your fans hope to get from you in terms of advice, tips, etc.?) By keeping a majority of your status updates focused away from you and your goal of selling books, you'll not only encourage interaction, but you'll be building a tribe of die-hard fans.

7. Leak info! Fans love to feel in the know. Give them a reason to visit your Facebook page by providing "leaked" cover art, story ideas, and news about new projects in the works.

8. Let fans read and critique. How do musicians build street teams and fan bases? They provide downloadable demos and free bumper stickers. They give the fans all they need to (a) love the band and (b) help promote it. So, don't be stingy with your writing! Get your words in front of your readers. Give them something to share with others, and ask for their input on character names, plot twists, and more. It may seem silly to you, but die-hard fans love this sort of thing.

9. Talk about other books/movies/TV shows in the same genre. This is a great tip for unpublished writers! Chances are, if people like *your* books, they'll like other books in the same genre. Keep an ongoing discussion somewhere on your page (could be the Notes section) where fans can gush or gripe over what other authors are doing in the genre. You may need to spearhead the conversation, which will mean reading those books and watching those movies and shows, but when was reading in your genre ever a bad thing?

10. Be yourself. I know it sounds cliché, but you'll have the best reaction from followers if you keep it casual and not try to turn it into some professional, stuffy experience. Keep things fun. Keep things focused on your fans, and you're good to go.

Building a Following

You have your page in place, and you have a plan for keeping fans active on it. But where do the fans come from? Apart from begging all of your Facebook friends to go over and "Like" your page (which you shouldn't do, by the way), how will people know your page exists? How will they find it? And what's their incentive for getting involved?

Here we go with another smattering of ideas!

7 Tips for Growing Your Facebook Author Community

1. Giveaways. I'm going to state the obvious here, but giveaways really can increase your reach if they're done right. The main thing is to have a list of hoops that entrants must jump through in order to qualify, such as "Liking" your Facebook page, sharing about your giveaway on Twitter and Facebook, etc. When fans meet your qualifications, enter them to win a free book or something of the sort. (For a list of giveaway prize ideas, jump ahead to the section on Goodreads). Of course, this strategy works for promoting most social media sites, and you're more than welcome to require that they follow you on Twitter, Pinterest, and Google+ while you're at it, but don't get too carried away. You don't want the process by which they enter the giveaway to outweigh the prize.

2. Bylines. You can Facebook your heart out, but sometimes the easiest way to get in front of new potential fans is to get your words in front of them via guest blogging, podcasting, and article-writing. This means finding blogs, podcasts, and e-zines that all cater to your ideal reader and then approaching them about providing content. Whenever you're taken up on the offer and your name appears elsewhere on the web, be sure to link to your Facebook group. Your byline can read something like this: Jane Doe is a contemporary romance author from Chicago, Illinois. Check her out on **Facebook** and **Twitter**. (Include appropriate hyperlinks.)

3. Street teams. A street team is a great way to mobilize people to tell their friends about your books. Put together a Facebook street team of your 25–100 (or so) most dedicated fans. Give them either a private group or a restricted Facebook page so that they can interact and build off one another's momentum and enthusiasm. Agree to provide them with the promo material they may need, including links to where you appear on the web, free books, and other alluring tchotchkes. In return, ask that they spread these things around the Internet and their schools, churches, workplaces, etc. Many times you can reward them with signed copies of your books and some Skype face time. Of course, there is a lot of other fun stuff you can do with street teams. There's really no end to the benefits of mobilizing fans to promote on your behalf.

4. Back cover copy. There's no reason that your Facebook URL, Twitter handle, and website info can't all show up somewhere in your book. Fight to have these things on the back cover or where your author bio is located, and at the very least, you can ask for ad space on the back pages. If you need to add this info into the manuscript yourself when you hand in the final draft, so be it. Things easily slip through the cracks in publishing, so be vigilant.

5. Promotional items. The same goes for postcards, bookmarks, and any other promotional pieces your publisher (or you) may provide. Include your social media info. And if you really want to get fancy, include a QR code on your promo materials that directs users to your website or Facebook group.

6. Create challenges for your fans. Challenge everyone to introduce your writing to someone new. Or challenge them to put the link to your page on their Facebook walls. The goal here is to use fan enthusiasm to your advantage. In turn, let those who participate read a chapter of an upcoming book or something simple yet meaningful.

7. Network at conferences, on blogs, forums, etc. One of the best results of attending a conference is that you'll come away with other writer friends. To make the most of this, don't be afraid to talk about what you're doing as a writer. Get people excited about your book. Then invite them to visit your Facebook page. (A bookmark or postcard would be a good handout at this point.) Some of the best conferences for this kind of networking are the ones that incorporate readers *and* writers. RT Booklovers, for example, is a huge romance conference that is packed with readers—each of them a potential fan.

Of course, one of the most surefire ways to gain fans is to make them an offer they can't refuse...

The Story of How I Gained 100 Followers in a Day
I'm a literary agent (duh). Consequently, there are authors and writers out there who are really interested in what I have to say. They respect my opinion on the industry, and since I've also established myself as a marketing person, they're interested in what I have to say regarding social media and author promotions.

Now, it's easy to forget that agents must promote themselves as well. Otherwise, if no one knew I existed, I wouldn't see any great projects come across my desk.

Keeping all of this in mind, I concocted a plan...

It started when I offered free social media critiques on our agency blog. Part of my reasoning was to be nice and help authors out, but I also wanted to gain trust and grow my agent platform.

The post was shared quite a bit on Twitter and through other venues, and the coolest part is that it attracted NEW readers to the blog. In exchange for a bit of my time, I got new readers, positioned myself as an expert, *and* got my name out among people who are not closely linked to me. Pretty cool. (Oh, and I also got free blog fodder for the rest of my life. Six months later, I'm still working through all those critiques.)

I received roughly 115 comments on this social media critique promo. That's around 100 people (some commented more than once) who not only interacted with me online, but who were then driven to come back every Thursday in hopes that their sites would be reviewed.

This strategy was a clear success, but it proved to be pretty time-consuming. So, I wanted something simpler. I refined my approach a bit, knowing I had something of a captive audience, and launched a new strategy to ring in 2013.

A few days before the launch, I announced that I was devising a plan to "give back." Then, on December 31, I posted this:

FREE ONE-LINER FEEDBACK!

As a token of appreciation for everyone who has "Liked" this page, I'd like to give you something in return.

1. Simply post your one-liner(s)/loglines/hooks below, and I'll message you my quick, initial thoughts (whether I'd ask to hear more, etc.). Please adhere to the rules of a typical logline: one sentence long, can be read in 10–30 seconds.

2. Please share this on your walls in case there are others out there who would like to take me up on this offer. (They simply have to "Like" my page and then leave a comment here!)

Wishing all of you a fabulous 2013! And hopefully, this will start the year off right.

Please share!

I had around 650 "Likes" on my rather-new Facebook page before the promo. In one day that number jumped to 750. My post was shared a whopping 85 TIMES on Facebook and even more so elsewhere. It saw 145 comments and was viewed by 1,572 people. This means that in a sense it went viral. It went well beyond its immediate reach of 650. That week my Facebook page reached 5,940 people. What's even cooler is my next big status ("What author, living or dead, would you have coffee with?") was seen by 2,028 people.

Craziness.

So, how does this apply to you?

It shows what you can do when you find what you're good at. It's something you can offer to your readers that they will gobble up. Simply ask yourself, "What am I good at? How can I take that and turn it into more fans?"

For some, this may be as simple as asking yourself what you do for a living and what skills you've learned on the job that others would appreciate.

Nonfiction authors should do this kind of thing ALL THE TIME. If you're working on a book on financial stability, for example, and you're certified and educated and have all your ducks in a row, offer simple things for free—things that you merely need to give an opinion on, things Suze Orman would offer.

This even applies if you've got a memoir. Let's say it's on your battle with cancer (which is the HARDEST type of book to sell, by the way). The fact is you're an expert on cancer. You're an expert on cancer etiquette and the various needs felt by the family and friends of the cancer patient. When people don't know what to say or do, you know EXACTLY how to fill that space. You're an expert among those people and those groups, and you could use that to grow your following—not just to help yourself, mind you, but to help others navigate that world.

Fiction authors can do this if their books tie in with their hobbies. Let's say you write a cozy mystery series that involves baking. Well, you can give away recipes or baking tips or you can answer baking questions for free. Or if your historical series takes place in France, you can set up an entire Francophiles Facebook page in which you fill the needs of all those France-obsessed potential readers out there.

Essentially, this strategy is about exploiting your "expertness" and then giving away the goods so that in return you're followed, "Liked," Tweeted, and shared.

Yes, it takes effort. Yes, it can be time-consuming. But nothing comes easy! And it's worth it.

A Note to Unpublished Authors on Facebook

If you're an unpublished, no-name author, it's going to be very hard to grow a following through Facebook, and in all honesty, it might be a better idea to pour your time and energy into blogging or speaking or writing articles. But that doesn't mean it's a lost cause. There ARE people out there who don't have books and yet manage to have decent followings, right? The rules are just a bit different for them, and it all starts with a shift in focus.

First, ignore the numbers. Did you hear me? Stop looking at your low "Likes" and follower numbers only to pout and complain. STOP IT! You're only hurting yourself. Instead, think of Facebook as a place where you can build your army. This is where you're going to find your die-hard fans—people who will do anything to champion your book and career. If they're excited enough to follow you when you don't have much to offer, they'll be that much more pumped when you have actual books on store shelves.

Second, the goal for an unpublished author (especially if they write fiction) should be to find 100–500 people who are total fans of you and your writing. I guarantee that the people willing to like your author page on Facebook without needing to see a final product from you are pretty close to qualifying as super-fans already.

Dispelling Professional Page Myths

Every once in awhile I receive some questions regarding professional Facebook pages. You see, there are a lot of rumors surrounding the professional page, and many will claim that it's self-sabotage to switch your following over from personal to a professional page. But I entirely disagree.

Let's take some time to dispel the **top 5 Facebook myths when it comes to using the site for marketing and promotions**.

Myth #1: The Professional Facebook Page makes promotions difficult because it only shows your updates to a third of your fan base.

This isn't necessarily true. Your fans have the power to choose how often they see your posts. If they want to view every post, they can select that option. If they only want to view the most popular posts, they can opt for that.

But let's get to the bottom of this myth. This statement is making the assumption that all of your posts in your *personal* profile are seen by ALL of your friends. This is not true. Go to your personal Facebook profile and think of a friend that you haven't heard or seen much of lately—one of those people that you wonder if maybe he or she has unfriended you. Now go look him or her up. Chances are that he or she has been posting quite frequently! But you haven't seen his or her posts. Why? Because not only do you have the power to filter your feeds, but Facebook sometimes selects which posts you view on your news feed and which are visible through other means on the site. And sometimes you don't see updates at all.

In other words, not all of your friends are seeing your posts, just like you aren't seeing all of their posts. Therefore, the argument that you are losing views by switching over to a professional page isn't a solid one. No matter where you house your professional Facebook presence, you aren't going to reach all of your followers.

Myth #2: You have to promote (which means spending money) any posts on your Professional Facebook Page that you want to gain traction.

This is absolutely untrue. The promotion option certainly helps, and it guarantees that your post will reach all of your fans. But it's also possible to go viral without having to shell out any money.

The one-liner Facebook promo I shared earlier didn't cost me a single cent. I used Tweets and regular Facebook posts to spread the word. I didn't even *consider* spending money to promote my offer. I figured it was solid enough to promote itself.

It shows you what old-fashioned, word-of-mouth marketing can get you.

Myth #3: Facebook is targeting and bullying those who use Facebook professionally.

Again, this is not entirely true. Remember, Facebook was not created for small businesses or marketing and promotions. It was originally created for students to be able to easily connect with one another. (You needed an .edu e-mail address to create an account at one time.) It has grown to accommodate users of all ages and vocations, and even businesses and corporations. However, its primary target market will always be the user who is connecting with friends, family, etc. So, any time Facebook seems to bully its corporate side, remember that it is doing so to protect the average user.

This is why businesses are encouraged to create a page instead of a personal profile. A business page separates the relationship between business owner and guest/customer in a way that protects both parties. How annoying would it be if you had to add PNC Bank as your friend instead of just being able to "Like" its corporate page?

If you have any ill feelings toward Facebook's treatment of you as an author, please put it aside. They're doing what they believe is best to protect the average user and prevent what could easily become a constant sales-pitch zone.

Myth #4: Facebook is being mean when they try to charge money for things.

Facebook is a business, much like your author career, and in my opinion they've done a good job of keeping it free. But just like you don't give away all of your books to your friends and family, Facebook shouldn't have to keep *everything* free. They need to be able to make money; otherwise, they will stop striving to make it a better user experience. (And if you think Facebook make too much money as it is, then I'd be interested to hear your feelings on the matter once you're a bestselling author.)

Myth #5: Facebook sucks, and Google+ is better.

Would fans of Google+ ever delete their Facebook accounts? Of course not. Why? Because that's where everyone is.

You may prefer Google+'s structure and usage system better, but it doesn't seem to be going anywhere fast. Facebook met a need at the right time and continues to be our number one social media site.

Does it suck? No. Personally, I'm grateful it exists. I know it has helped me grow my agent platform, and I'm sure it's helped you in your author career, too. When I can say the same thing about Google+, then that will be the time to decide which one I prefer. But for now, if you don't like Facebook, then don't spend your time there. It's as simple as that.

8
MISCELLANEOUS SOCIAL MEDIA SITES

If you haven't noticed or been to the social media circus for very long, social media sites and fads come and go. I mean, remember MySpace?

When a site gets fairly popular, everyone feels they need to go check it out, which is fine. But spending time on a social media site doesn't mean you should include it as one of your promotional hubs. Let me explain...

Pinterest exploded in 2012. Suddenly, everyone was pinning their hearts out, and I had lots of authors feel as though they needed to have a strong Pinterest presence. But they didn't have a clue what they would pin or how those pins would result in fans or sales. While they enjoyed Pinterest and were having fun on the site, they were creating unnecessary stress for themselves as they struggled to make their time on Pinterest profitable.

Just because you spend personal time on a social media site does NOT mean you must also spend professional time there.

Let me repeat, but in **bolded font...**

If you like a site for personal reasons, that doesn't mean you have to also use it professionally—even if everyone, including the top marketing person in the nation, is gushing about how great it is to use professionally. Just don't go there. Don't make social media a chore. If you enjoy a site but can't really figure out how to make it work for you professionally, then let that be your answer.

Pinterest, LinkedIn, and Google+ are just a few of the social media sites that I don't feel a great need to push on authors. Their usage is minimal, their markets are niche, and their options are limited. But while we're at this whole platform thing, I figured I should spend some time at least touching on *some* of these sites.

PINTEREST

Social media sites come and go, and Pinterest is the most recent site to see a major usage spike. Consequently, businesses and brands and marketing teams are feeling the pressure to infiltrate the site and use it for their evil purposes of getting you to buy, want, and *need* things or experiences that you normally could care less about. (I know for a fact this is true. I used to be one of those big, bad brand marketers, having to answer to a boss who pushed us to infiltrate social media space simply because "everyone was doing it.")

Whenever something is new and fresh, there will naturally be a buzz in the beginning about how to use it for personal gain. This certainly rings true for Pinterest, since many authors have jumped on the pinning bandwagon.

Let's be clear about what Pinterest is: Pinterest is a site that allows users to "pin" images found on the web to their virtual pinboards. There's minimal text involved because it's a visual site. It's all about virtual scrapbooking and visual inspiration. To give an even better idea of what/how Pinterest is used, I'd say right now it's probably the biggest fad among brides-to-be. They can have their wedding pinboards where they gather all of the pretty photos they see online and then use them as wedding inspiration.

So, why are authors feeling the pressure? I honestly

can't say, and if you're reading this, baffled by corporate America's desire to turn Pinterest into a marketing trap, then you and I can have a drink sometime and shake our heads at marketing teams who feel they *have* to have all of these online presences. Personally, I wouldn't waste my time with Pinterest. I think it's a fad that will fade, and your time would be better spent with more tried-and-true sites.

But if you *must* do some professional pinning, here are some ideas:

1. Create a pinboard of your book covers. People are very visual, so what better use for Pinterest than to gather all of your book covers (provided you're a multi-published author) and put them on a pinboard? Be sure to label the board and the pins, using great genre-esque keywords. Then fans may stumble across the board, follow it, and maybe, just maybe, buy some of your backlisted books. This is a great way to promote old titles and *hopefully* get them circulating around the Internet. (You may even want to ask fans to re-pin, or you could create a contest that encourages them to do so.)

2. Create a "novel inspiration" pinboard. Novel characters are usually inspired by celebrities, and settings are inspired by real places. Why not tease your fans by creating a pinboard that holds a bunch of photos of people and locations that inspired your upcoming book? This would also be a great thing to pass on to your publishing house's design team. It would give them some help when creating the perfect book cover. (I've also heard of authors looking to their fans to help "cast the roles" of their favorite characters. It's a neat game, for sure.)

3. Create a novel comparison pinboard. This can especially work for unpublished authors. Think of the authors within your genre who write stories similar to your own. Gather their book covers, author photos, and whatnots, and put them on a pinboard. This can be your "If you like _____, you'll also like my book!" board. (If you have a published book, be sure to add it to the pinboard as well!) You never know when it might hook some potential fans.

4. Create an upcoming cover art pinboard. Fans love leaked images, so when you begin working through cover designs with your publisher (or even if you e-publish!), be sure to "leak" the images to your pinboard. Ask for fan input and make them feel part of the process. Plus, Pinterest is designed to make it easy for users to share images. If you start seeing your book's cover appear on multiple boards, you know you've got a winner. (Again, this is a prime idea for a contest.)

5. Create a blog pinboard. Some authors see success with Pinterest when they consistently pin photos from their blog posts. This requires you to (a) maintain a blog, (b) include photos with each post, and (c) properly pin those photos. But the general idea is that if you end up with some photos that attract attention, people will click through to see where they originated. That's how they end up on your blog!

6. Encourage wish lists. This is an idea I stole from the clothing store, Express. During the 2012 holiday season, they offered a shopping spree to one lucky Pinner who put together an Express wish list. As of when this was written, Pinterest's search engine was totally unreliable, so if you do this idea you'll need to develop some sort of way in which Pinners can let you know their boards exist. But the basic idea is that you ask Pinners to create holiday (or Valentine's Day, etc.) wish lists in which they pin books that they want, including some of yours. One lucky winner will receive a prize. The ultimate payoff with this tactic is that it encourages family and friends of these Pinners to actually go out and purchase some of these wish list items as gifts. That's what happened to me. I made my Express pinboards, and though I didn't win anything, I received three Express items that holiday season from family and friends.

Proper Pinning 101

- Create great, concise descriptions of each pin, using hashtags, keywords, links, and more.
- Pin book covers from sites in which the book can actually

be purchased.

- Tag every book cover pin with genre, author, and title information.

TUMBLR

I discussed blogging in a previous chapter, but there's also something called microblogging, and it's pretty cool.

Microblogging is exactly what it sounds like—it's a smaller, more condensed form of blogging. Images are usually the focus of such microblogs, but they can also be text-based. Typically, they're used for humor. Someone gets a funny idea, and they create a microblog around that idea, providing content on a fairly regular basis. These "funny ideas" are more commonly known as "memes."

Here are some of my favorite microblogs:

- KateMiddletonForTheWin.Tumblr.com—I have a major girl crush on Kate, but these make me laugh every time.

- SlushPileHell.tumblr.com—I wish I would have thought of this first.

- ClientsFromHell.net—Maybe it's my marketing background that makes this microblog so appealing?

Most microblogs use Tumblr as their site's service provider. It's really the leading host for this approach to blogging.

Why should authors care about microblogging?

1. It's quick. Constructing a traditional blog post can take hours, depending on how finicky you are. Microblogging takes a fraction of that time, using a fraction of those words. Of course, for some of the comedically challenged, it may take *more* brainpower. So again, know your own limits.

2. It's focused. I know I keep hounding you about having a goal, but microblogging is a great example of a medium that simply won't work without a goal. It practically forces you to choose a topic, preventing you from microblogging about flowers one day, Mozart the next, then your dog, and then your deep thoughts on black holes followed by a reposted tribute to

AC/DC.

3. It's clean. No fancy backgrounds. No design expertise needed. Just clean and simple—ideal for the digital n00b.

4. It's friendly. Admit it, sometimes you skim or ignore blog posts from even your most favorite authors and bloggers simply because you don't have time for them. Microblogging requires such a small commitment from readers that it very nearly guarantees your readers will be checking out each post.

How can Tumblr and microblogging grow your author platform?

Think about what you write. Think really deeply about it. Ask yourself…

- What's my genre?
- Who reads what I write?
- What stage of life are they in?
- What hobbies do my characters have that could also appeal to the target reader?
- What unique elements/themes/storylines are in my book?

Answer these questions, and you'll start to see the beginnings of a great microblog. For example, let's answer them with heartwarming or small town fiction in mind:

- **What's my genre?** Heartwarming/Small Town Fiction
- **Who reads what I write?** Women, ages 35–60
- **What stage of life are they in?** Married, moms, approaching retirement. Some have lots of free time, others have limited free time. But each reader is looking to find/maintain/rediscover her personal interests.
- **What hobbies do my characters have that could also appeal to the target reader?** Quilting, baking, horses
- **What unique elements/themes/storylines are in my book?** Cowboys/farm boys, small town girl/boy in big city and vice versa, etc.

Based on these answers alone, you could develop a number of microblogs, provided that you can gather the content needed to highlight cowboys, quilting, baking, or any of the other leads. If you don't have access to horses or know anything about quilting, then you're limited. But the goal is to extract themes, hobbies, and lifestyle ideals from your novel and develop microblogs that speak to them visually and/or textually.

Or you could just come up with some sort of hilarious meme that has nothing to do with your book or writing, gain a following, and then somehow *maybe* get them interested in your book. Of course, this strategy works best if you in turn write some sort of comedic fiction.

GOODREADS

NOTE: Some of this information comes from author Jennifer Murgia, and it's geared a bit more toward those who are on their way to being published (whether with a big house, a small house, a digital house, or something they're doing on their own).

Goodreads.com is a reader's social haven. Here you'll find bookworms, virtual librarians, discussion groups, and a complete online cataloging system catered just for you. It's an easy way to keep track of the books you're reading, want to read, and have read, along with a place to share what you think. For an author, this is a promotional wonderland, because this is where readers congregate.

Goodreads pulls book info from Amazon, meaning if you're published, your book is already in the Goodreads database. Once you have a Goodreads account, you can link it to your book, but **being an author on this particular social media site has clear promotional benefits**:

1. Personal information on whom you're reaching. Goodreads provides personalized stats on everything from your book's reviews to your author fan base. Handy graphs allow you to view your reach over time and even pinpoint successful (or unsuccessful) marketing efforts.

2. A specialized profile that goes above and beyond. Goodreads authors are allowed to add videos and events to their profiles. They can also sync them with their blogs, creating a true destination for fans. Additional benefits include participation in panels and discussions, as well as unique advertising opportunities. These features are not available to non-author users, so author profiles really have become a key part of the Goodreads experience.

3. Worry-free giveaway options. The site has everything in place to make book giveaways simple. From detailed legalese and clear rules to a separate "space" where readers flock to see what books are available, Goodreads has it covered. It's really as simple as filling out the form and then following through when you have your winner(s).

The advantages of Goodreads go beyond these three things, as it also allows you to more easily discover potential fans (and vice versa). The site is crawling with thousands upon thousands of reader groups, who have banned together based on genre preference or hobbies or other lifestyle similarities. Of all of these "miscellaneous" social media sites, I'd recommend Goodreads as one to look into.

Success with Goodreads

As with any social media site, the question of *how* to make Goodreads a success once you have all your components in place is still a valid one.

5 Steps to Build Book Hype on Goodreads

1. Participate. Just like any social media site, Goodreads requires participation in order for the magic to happen. The first step is to be a regular Goodreads participant. This means reviewing books, tracking your book reading progress, adding books to your shelves, commenting on friends' shelves and statuses, and getting comfortable with how the site works and how people use it. For any Goodreads virgin looking to use it for personal promotion, I think it would be helpful to spend a month or two learning the ropes. Don't just dive into it with the intention of selling books. Figure out what does and doesn't work from a user's perspective. Follow a few of your favorite authors and see what THEY do. Learning and participating are the first steps.

2. Maintain your author page. Treat your page as you would your author website. Dump book trailers, blog posts, and information onto your Goodreads author page as often as you can. You can even use both of those mediums (video and blog) to interact with fans, make announcements, and more. Before you start promoting yourself, you want this page to be full of information so that you don't appear to be a ghost author.

3. Host a giveaway. The steps to hosting a giveaway are pretty self-explanatory on the site. You simply go to "Giveaways," click "List a Book," and fill out the fields. This is an important component of the Goodreads experience because it gets your book in front of lots and lots of potential buyers. Sure, most of them are there to try and snag a free read, but BELIEVE ME when I say that free books mean more sales.

I've heard conflicting information on how many copies to give away and how long to run the promotion, and I lean toward agreeing with the research that shows giving away one book in a shortened span of time (5 days or so) works best. But you can always experiment and dial it in for your readers.

The idea, though, is that people will add your book to their lists as "to-read." So, even if they don't win a copy, that book will still be there, taunting them. Eventually, some will go and buy the book.

4. Join groups. There are a number of author and reader groups on Goodreads, and you can even create a fan club for you or your book. These are like the forums and message boards of old where people with similar interests would congregate and chat. Use this to your advantage. Simply figure out who your ideal readers are and befriend them. Eventually, they'll realize you're an author and buy your book.

Whatever you do, don't spam them with "I'M AN AUTHOR; BUY MY BOOK." Just be nice and engaging, and when the time is right, you can mention you have a book. But relationships come first.

5. Make friends and interact with readers. That is really the secret. Yes, it's a time sink, and yes, it will require long-term commitment. But so does your author career. Suck it up, cupcake, and get out there! Make friends and then put those friends to "work," asking them to review, list, and share your book. Many will be happy to oblige.

So, we've gotten into some giveaway specifics, but what if you want to run a giveaway on your own, apart from Goodreads? I've got some thoughts...

How to Host a Successful Book Giveaway

Book giveaways happen all the time. Whether through Goodreads, at a conference, over the radio during an author interview, or at a book signing, hundreds of free books are given away every day. The goal behind these giveaways is to generate interest and a hope that the person receiving the book will (a) read it, (b) love it, and (c) talk about it, resulting in (d) money in the author's and publisher's pockets.

But with so many books being handed out daily, how many authors are actually seeing any of those results? The answer would be the ones who **go about giveaways the smart way**:

1. Plan in advance. This isn't a seat-of-your-pants affair. I don't care how busy you are or whether you gravitate toward chaos over organization. The best way to ensure success with your giveaway is to start planning well ahead of time. We're talking 2–3 months, depending on if it's timed with a book release (and will therefore need a bit more TLC). The goal here is to have room to get the chips in place.

2. Give your giveaway plenty of time. For KDP giveaways on Amazon (in which you offer your book for free), I've found it's best to use up all of your five days at once. Conversely, I've heard that though Goodreads suggests you hold your giveaway for a month, the week-long giveaways tend to have the same results. On average, I'd suggest that you give your readers 5–10 days to finalize their entries before you choose a winner—no matter where or how you're housing your giveaway. This will give your book more time in the spotlight, while it also pushes readers to take action and complete the entry steps

3. Research, research, research. Spend time identifying what blogs, forums, message boards, and online groups would be interested in your book. Keep detailed records of these groups and try to jump in (creating a profile if necessary) as soon as you can. You want to have a presence in these places before you do the drive-by advertisement. This is a much more delicate matter than it sounds. The idea is to NOT come across as some money- or sales-hungry author, but instead you want to come across as an author who simply wants readers to know that there's a giveaway going on that could interest them.

4. Choreograph an epic web presence for *each day* of your giveaway. This means:

- Having guest blog posts pop up all over on friends' and fans' blogs

- Writing an aggressive Twitter campaign in which you have set Tweets for each day of the giveaway

- Requesting that friends, fans, and family members with large platforms reTweet, repost, or share any information you ask them to (agree to do the same for them if you need leverage)

- Frequenting each of those URLs that you researched (in the above step) and letting those groups know that you've got a book giveaway going on and that you'd love for them to participate

- Putting links on Facebook, Pinterest, and wherever else you may have a following of friends or fans

Basically, you want the world to know that your giveaway is occurring.

5. Request something from entrants. Don't just ask them to post a comment or send you an e-mail to enter. Make them "Like" your Facebook page, follow you on Twitter, and whatever else you think would be useful to your overall author promotional strategies. Of course, if you request that they

Tweet or Facebook about the giveaway, be sure to spell out what exactly you'd like them to say. (I hate to be Captain Obvious here, but the message should be directly related to encouraging others to enter the giveaway.) Be sure to have them mention your Twitter handle in their Tweets, so that you can keep track of who is following through, and have them message you links to other places on the Internet where they posted a link to your giveaway. In a nutshell, make them work for that free book by spreading the word about the giveaway.

6. Stay active in the space. If you announce your giveaway on your blog, then be sure to not only be active in the Comments section, but structure subsequent days' blog posts around the giveaway as well. There's just nothing more dissuading than to visit a giveaway post only to feel as though the author has abandoned it and moved on. You want it to be an active giveaway-focused space, as this encourages participation and buzz.

7. Announce winners when you say you'll announce winners. Seems pretty obvious, but you'd be surprised.

8. Follow through with entrants by visiting their blogs, following them on Twitter, and ANYTHING else to get them to remember who you are after the drawing is over. This will keep you top of mind, making them more likely to talk about and/or buy your book.

9. Push for reviews. Whether your winners love the book or not is beside the point. (I've never heard of one-star reviews deterring a purchase UNLESS the rating is due to poorly edited material.) Maximize the giveaway by requesting that the winners write a review for the book on Amazon and Goodreads. This way, if you have multiple winners, you get something out of it.

10. Don't stop now. The worst thing you can do is disappear after the giveaway. Tease entrants by announcing either another giveaway that will start in x amount of time, or offer them some additional value that will keep them coming back to your blog or site. This could be as simple as a note saying, "No worries if you didn't win this one! In a few days I'll

be offering a free Chapter One sample of my debut novel..."
The goal here is to be in their line of vision long term.

Giveaways aren't only for books. Many authors advertise
other kinds of prizes to really draw new readers.

10 Prize Ideas That Won't Cost You a Fortune

1. Gift cards
2. Coupons for e-books (could be novellas, shorts, etc., that you have self-published)
3. The chance to name a character in an upcoming book (may only work for established authors)
4. Twenty-minute Skype call with the author
5. Free book
6. A book dedication
7. A shout-out in the Acknowledgements section
8. A "fan of the year" or "fan of the month" badge for his or her blog/website
9. Book doodads in the form of PDFs that you e-mail to winners, such as paper dolls (for children's or romance genres), detailed world maps (for speculative fiction genres), recipes (for historical genres, etc.), paper crafts/Cubeecrafts (for children's or speculative genres)—basically anything that appeals to readers, their children/grandchildren, or the inner nerd or hobbyist.
10. Themed gift baskets that tie in with your novel, such as gardening-theme baskets for gardening cozy mysteries, etc.

YOUTUBE

There are different ways you can use video as a tool for promoting your author career or books. There's the book trailer, the pitch video, the vlog (video blog), and the study guide-type of video (often used in reading groups, church groups, classrooms, etc.).

I'm sure there are other avenues, but these stand out to me as having the most potential. Let's look at each one in depth.

Book Trailers

We've all been to the movies. We've all seen movie trailers. Book trailers are no different. They're 30-second (roughly) advertisements for your book. They focus on the book's hook and should connect the audience with no more than three characters (hero, heroine, villain/obstacle). To get an idea of what a GREAT book trailer looks like, you may want to look up the trailer for Ally Condie's *Matched*. It's a bit more hi-tech than others, but even then, it's simplistic in that it doesn't use live-action scenes. It uses catchy design techniques to create a sophisticated look.

Author Conlan Brown does his own trailers. Granted, he's educated in film, but he does trailers on his own without the help of a studio or lots of extra marketing dollars. Google him sometime.

If you don't trust your trailer-making abilities, you may want to consider hitting up the local college. For a few hundred dollars, I'm sure you could employ a student to do your bidding.

Pitch Videos

Pitch videos are 1–2 minute videos that can be used when pitching your book to an agent or editor. A few of my authors have employed this technique, and I see it as a great way to help your audience feel comfortable with you and interested in your project.

Your pitch video should include information about you and your story. It doesn't have to be polished or perfect. Stock photography and scripted lines are okay. No one will be expecting you to bust out an Oscar-winning performance here. Just be yourself and express your passion for the craft or your knowledge of the topic (if nonfiction).

Vlogs

As an author in the twenty-first century, it's important to connect with your readers. Video blogs are ways in which you can break out of the samey-same blog mold and provide something different. The rules for these are similar to blogging rules:

- Stay on topic.

- Keep the conversation moving (no rambling or super long stories allowed!).

- Think about the visual/auditory experience. There should be a reason you're vlogging and not blogging. Your content needs to have some sort of visual or auditory payoff for the viewer.

- Have fun and be entertaining. This is essential because people can't skim through a video like they can a blog post. Once you lose them, they're gone.

- Keep it concise. We're talking two minutes max. Beyond that, you start to lose people.

Study Guide-Type Videos

Clearly, I didn't quite know what to call these types of videos, but they're what you get when an author writes a nonfiction book and then offers some kind of supporting video experience—usually for educational or training purposes. Sometimes these videos are offered for sale as a DVD, but that usually only happens if your book takes off. If you feel that having free online discussion-type videos would help you in your promotions, then it could be worth it to put them together yourself.

Basically, all that you do is write a script for every chapter of your book (or so). The script should bring new light to the principles covered in your book. In other words, it should enhance the reading experience, not take away from or repackage it. Pay a local film crew to shoot the videos and put them together. (The videos should not be longer than 10–20 minutes each.) Then put them online. I think you'll find it much easier to peddle your book if you have a freebie like this in your back pocket. For whatever reason, it's easier to tell people about your book when you feel you're doing them a favor by offering them something that sweetens the deal.

Putting Your Videos to Work

Okay, so you have your book trailer ready to go. Now what? Well, it's not rocket science, as it's pretty similar to the rules for any other social media site. Here are **5 Ways to Ensure Readers Watch Your Videos:**

1. Put links to your videos on your website, your Goodreads page, your Facebook, etc.

2. Title the videos using lots of nouns. "Frankenstein by Mary Shelley OFFICIAL book trailer; Genre: Horror." The video's title doesn't have to flow or be read aloud. It just has to be searchable. All those awesome nouns help with searchability.

3. Embed videos in your blog posts. It's one thing to say, "Hey, I have a YouTube Channel!" It's another to put the videos directly into your blog posts or on your Facebook wall. It's so much easier to click "play" when users don't have to click through a series of links first.

4. Promise a giveaway when a video reaches x number of views. This gets people sharing the video, but that means the giveaway either needs to be really great or the video needs to be super entertaining. No one wants to share a dull video.

5. Create videos for specific groups. This is a method that I haven't seen many authors do, and yet I feel it's the most foolproof. The idea is that you identify gatherings of what you would consider your book's ideal readers. For example, if you write Christian teen fiction, your ideal audience would be church kids. You then target this audience with a video tailored to them. You figure out what kinds of videos youth groups typically show, and then mimic that with a video of your own. Can you imagine the potential awesomeness if you were to send your youth group-ready bumper video or book trailer out to 100 youth pastors and asked them to show it during youth group? You'd have to include a letter and also a message of *why* teens need to read your book, but still. This is the type of marketing that could really work.

Now what?

Okay, so you're familiar with the various types of videos that can be used to promote yourself or your book, and you even know a bit about *how* to bring it together. But is it worth it? Videos don't come cheap, and to end up with a great finished product, it's going to take lots of time. So, are these tools worthwhile?

Like any online marketing tool, videos are as effective as you want them to be. Left to their own devices, they won't receive many views (unless they become viral hits). But paired with an aggressive promotional plan, they can reach new readers in ways that blog posts, Tweets, and message board threads cannot. Videos just tend to be much more sharable than most things, probably because we're programmed to want to *watch* instead of *read* or *listen*.

I've encouraged a few of my authors to not think of their book trailers as sales tools but instead as a method of generating buzz and discussion around their books.

Now, after saying all this, I want to also point out that videos are not a MUST. No one is going to *make* you have a trailer (unless you promised in your proposal that you'd have one), and your blog readers aren't going to one day band together and demand a vlog from you.

A good rule of thumb is to think of your readership. If you write fiction for young adults, then yes, videos may be worthwhile investments. If you write historical romance, then not so much. Think about your audience before taking the plunge. And at the end of the day, if you're just not into the whole video thing, that's fine. Like I've said before, it's better to put your energy toward social media strategies that you're comfortable with and excited about than to spin your wheels on something that causes you concern.

LINKEDIN

Everyone who is on Facebook or Twitter or a similar social

media site has that *moment* where your boss or coworker links up with you online. Suddenly, your personal life isn't so personal, and things that you'd never think about saying, doing, sharing at work are under threat.

This is where LinkedIn swoops in and saves the day. Unlike the other social media sites we've mentioned, whose purposes are either to entertain or encourage keeping in touch with friends and family, LinkedIn's goal is for users to keep in touch with their professional contacts. So, that first boss you had in high school or that professor in college who liked your work or that client at that one job who was always a big fan? LinkedIn is for *those* people. Because hey, it's a lot less threatening to connect on a professional level than it is a personal one.

Lots of authors want to know about LinkedIn—how to use it, whether it's any good, how it helps authors. And to be honest, I'm a bit stumped. I don't see this medium as being a hidden treasure trove of potential readers. There's no easy way to peddle your goods, and those who try to treat it like Facebook (where they're always updating their profiles or statuses) just come across as a bit weird.

So, what *is* it good for?

I'd say it's more of a tool for a publishing professional, and here's what I mean by that:

1. LinkedIn could be the new Rolodex. Sure, now we have smartphones and online address books and other ways to organize all those contacts we make in the business world, but LinkedIn really takes it up a notch and provides you with all the info you need to know about someone's professional life. I could see how many are ditching other methods of connecting with professionals in favor of the "I'll find you on LinkedIn" approach. And with LinkedIn, there's no fear of losing that person's contact info, or for that matter, forgetting what they look like. Cool, huh?

2. LinkedIn could be the new résumé-filtering service. I know some businesses look to LinkedIn when they want to learn more about a potential hire, as profiles display everything from job history to key skills to education and organization affiliations.

3. LinkedIn could be the new interview process. LinkedIn has two neat features that really play to job interviews. First, it has a Recommendation feature that allows former coworkers, bosses, and professors to write an official recommendation that is viewable from your profile. The second feature is the Endorsements section where your current contacts can endorse you for the various skills you've claimed to possess. This is a great way for a potential employer (agent, publisher, editor, etc.) to sift through your professional résumé and get a feel for what *others* think.

4. LinkedIn could change the way publishing professionals interact. But it hasn't yet, and it's been running for some years now. So, I personally wouldn't spend too much time making sure all your LinkedIn ducks are in a row. Do what you can, when you can, and leave it at that.

Some Basic LinkedIn Rules to Follow when Linking Up with Publishing Professionals

1. Only connect with professionals you've met or worked with. There are differing schools of thought on this. Some treat LinkedIn as they would Facebook in that everyone is fair game, and if you have the slightest thing in common, it's worth connecting. Others treat LinkedIn as a sacred place where they only connect with those they know, trust, and can stand behind. I belong to the latter group, because I think it's the recommendation aspect that sets LinkedIn apart from other social media sites. I want to trust that when I see there is only two degrees of separation between me and someone else, that it's a sign of a *true,* real-life connection between my LinkedIn contact and this person I'm stalking.

Now, there is a tendency among authors to want to connect with every publisher, agent, and industry pro they can. Even if they fall into the latter category of treating LinkedIn as a sacred place, they feel that "publishing" itself is a strong enough connection and "Hey! What if connecting with this random editor on LinkedIn lands me a book deal?!" But I really don't think that's the way to go.

As an agent, I frequently receive connection requests from people I've never met. But, *because* I'm an agent, and because I feel my word means something (to some people) in the business, I ignore those requests. I want my LinkedIn connections to be with others that I know and trust. Should a publishing professional see that I'm connected to so-and-so author, I want them to feel better about that author and not wonder if I'm only connected to that person because of an overeager socialization process. In other words, I want each of my connections to be a sort of recommendation in and of itself. I realize that some users accept any connection sent to them, and that's fine. But there are others like me who take LinkedIn very seriously (as it's meant to be taken) and are particular about our connections.

2. Only ask for recommendations from those you've worked with for long periods of time. LinkedIn has this cool feature where others can write up a recommendation for you. It's tempting to want to use this to get a bunch of professional endorsements. But! There is some etiquette that goes along with that: (a) be sure you've worked at length with the person from whom you're asking the recommendation, (b) be sure he or she is the appropriate person to speak to your strengths and weaknesses, (c) don't hound him or her for a recommendation—ask once, then leave it alone—and (d) don't be offended if the recommendation isn't as glowing as you'd hoped.

3. Realize that these connections are just that—connections. Being connected with editors and agents does not guarantee anything. That's what a great book idea, solid writing, and an impressive platform are for.

A Success Story

I did hear from one author who claimed LinkedIn was the reason she could sell as many books as she did. Apparently, she had it down to a science, and she really utilized not only her connections, but also her knowledge of her connections' workplaces and strengths. It may sound creepy and stalkerish to be tracking your connections so thoroughly, but I can see how that could be effective. If you write pop culture nonfiction and suddenly realize you're connected with a bunch of college professors, then you have an automatic "in" with universities and classrooms.

I must admit the conversation left me more than skeptical (as did her spot on the panel in which she urged authors to sell books out of the trunks of their cars). But just like clockwork, after the conference (in which we'd had a very brief conversation), she sent me a connection request. I didn't accept it. Again, I really want my connections to *matter*. But I probably should have gone along with it just to figure out what the heck she does with LinkedIn that makes it so worthwhile.

Recapping the Miscellaneous Sites

Believe it or not, we've barely begun to touch on all of the social media opportunities available. It's just a constantly evolving space that is impossible to stay on top of if it's not your full-time job. So, I'll say it again: don't feel as though you have to do it all. Start small, and grow as you're able. Then stop when you're feeling full. It's as simple as that.

AFTERWORD

Well, you made it. You trudged through my collection of ideas and tips and thoughts and randomness and are on the other side. Hopefully, you feel empowered as you realize you really *can* do it. You can figure this whole thing out and make it work. You can be an online *extrovert* even if you're an in-person introvert. Yay!!!! This is huge! Throw yourself a party, or in true introvert fashion, reward yourself by curling up with a book.

More than anything, I hope this sparked some ideas of your own. I hope that as you read my overflow of ideas, you came away with things that seem do-able and simple and things you can enact without having to think too hard or worry too much.

I realize this was a super short look at social media, and while on one hand you're feeling overloaded and maxed out, there is still a side of you that is brimming with questions and what-ifs and thoughts and areas of confusion (because despite trying very hard to speak plainly, things don't always come out right).

So, I want you to know I'm here for you. If you come away from this with burning questions that can't be easily solved with a bit of extra research, drop me a note at ExtrovertedWriter@gmail.com. I'd be happy to try and help you as best I can.

ACKNOWLEDGMENTS

Thanks to Chip MacGregor for encouraging me to write this book. Thanks to all of the readers of Thursdays with Amanda. Thanks to Kyle Waalen for a great copyedit and Kimberly Appletwhite of Applewhite Designs for a fab cover.

And thanks to that boring social media job I held for three years. Because of it, and because of all I learned while there, I've been able to help the befuddled, introverted writers of the world understand online marketing.

ABOUT THE AUTHOR

Amanda Luedeke is a literary agent with MacGregor Literary, Inc. Her background is in social media marketing—a job in which she strategized and plotted world domination on behalf of her clients. She lives in Fort Wayne, Indiana, with her husband and Great Dane, Helo. She'd love to connect with you online.

Find her online:
Twitter: @AmandaLuedeke
Facebook: facebook.com/AgentAmandaLuedeke
Blog: Amanda blogs every Thursday at ChipMacgregor.com

Made in the USA
Charleston, SC
27 August 2014